# Employment and Shared Growth

# Employment and Shared Growth

## Rethinking the Role of Labor Mobility for Development

*Edited by*
Pierella Paci
Pieter Serneels

**THE WORLD BANK**
**Washington, DC**

1818 H Street, NW
Washington, DC 20433
Telephone: 202-473-1000
Internet: www.worldbank.org
E-mail: feedback@worldbank.org

ISBN-10:  0-8213-7107-X
ISBN-13:  978-0-8213-7107-7
e-ISBN-10:  0-8213-7108-8
e-ISBN-13:  978-0-8213-7108-4
DOI: 10.1596/978-0-8213-7107-7

**Library of Congress Cataloging-in-Publication Data**

Employment and shared growth : rethinking the role of labor mobility for development / [edited by] Pierella Paci, Pieter Serneels.
    p. cm.—(Directions in development)
    Papers presented at a June, 2006 conference organized by the Poverty Reduction and Development Effectiveness Department (PRMPR) of the World Bank (WB), in collaboration with the Labor Markets Team in the Social Protection group (HDNSP).
    Includes bibliographical references and index.
    ISBN-13: 978-0-8213-7107-7
    ISBN-10: 0-8213-7107-X
    ISBN-10: 0-8213-7108-8 (electronic)
    1. Labor supply—Developing countries—Congresses. 2. Manpower policy—Developing countries—Congresses. 3. Poverty—Developing countries—Congresses. I. Paci, Pierella, 1957- II. Serneels, Pieter M. (Pieter Maria), 1967- III. World Bank.

    HD5852.S617 2007
    331.12'042091724—dc22

                                                                           2007011291

# Contents

## Figures

## Tables

# Foreword

Labor is the most abundant asset of the poor, and in low-income countries what distinguishes the poor from the nonpoor is, for the most part, access to productive employment. Thus the quality and quantity of employment opportunities are increasingly recognized as one of the main transmission channels between growth and poverty reduction. It is therefore not surprising that creating "good" jobs for the poor is a fast-growing priority in the policy agenda of developing countries. However, the understanding by policy makers and their advisors of the mechanisms that make employment an effective transmission channel between growth and poverty reduction remains somewhat limited.

The Poverty Reduction and Development Effectiveness Department (PRMPR) of the World Bank, in collaboration with the Labor Markets Team in the Social Protection Group, organized the conference "Rethinking the Role of Jobs for Shared Growth," held in Washington, DC, in June 2006. It marked the beginning of a renewed effort by the Bank to improve the understanding of how these mechanisms operate and of the policy levers that may enhance their effectiveness.

This edited volume brings together the papers presented at the conference. The common theme is that of mobility in the labor market. As growth is related to sectoral shifts in economic activity, the mobility of labor plays a crucial role in ensuring sustainable growth whose benefits are shared amongst all individuals. The papers in this volume focus on selected priority issues at the frontier of research in the microeconomics of labor markets in developing countries, multisegmented labor markets, the role of informal employment and self-employment, the effect of worker mobility on income, and the impact of firm dynamics on growth and employment. These are important parts of the puzzle and contribute to a better understanding of the role of employment in the economic development of low-income countries.

*Luca Barbone*
*Director*
*Poverty Reduction and Development Effectiveness Department*
*The World Bank*

# Acknowledgments

This edited volume brings together papers presented at the conference "Rethinking the Role of Jobs for Shared Growth" organized by the Poverty Reduction and Development Effectiveness Department (PRMPR) of the World Bank in collaboration with the Labor Markets Team in the Social Protection Unit (HDNSP), in Washington, DC, in June 2006. Both the conference and this volume have benefited from the invaluable contributions of the participants and of many other colleagues.

We gratefully acknowledge the input of Peter Peek, Martin Rama, William Maloney, and Stefano Scarpetta (discussants) and the participation of Robert Holzmann, Michal Rutkowski, Mayra Buvinic, and Sudhir Shetty to the lively panel discussion that concluded the conference and shed further light on the issues raised in the presentations. We would also like to thank Danny Leipziger, Vice President, Luca Barbone, Sector Director, and Louise Cord, Sector Manager, for participating in the conference, for their input of ideas, and mostly for their continuous support of this initiative. We would also like to thank Stephen McGroarty and Mark Ingebretsen in the Bank's Office of the Publisher for their help and patience in bringing this book to the press. Finally, our thanks go to Nelly Obias and Jessica Ardinoto for their support throughout the process and to our colleagues in PRMPR and HDNSP, especially Edmundo Murrugarra, Catalina Gutierrez, Margo Hoftijzer, Katy Hull, and Angeli Kirk.

# Contributors

**Gary S. Fields** is professor of labor economics and economic development at Cornell University. His research focuses on labor markets and income distribution in developing countries. He has worked in Africa, Latin America, Asia, and Europe. His current projects are on empirical studies of income mobility and theoretical models of labor market policy. He holds B.A., M.A., and Ph.D. degrees in Economics from the University of Michigan.

**John Haltiwanger** received his Ph.D. from the Johns Hopkins University in 1981. After serving on the faculty of UCLA and Johns Hopkins, he joined the faculty of the University of Maryland in 1987. He served as chief economist of the U.S. Census Bureau from 1997–99. He is a research associate of the Center for Economic Studies at the Census Bureau and of the National Bureau of Economic Research. He is also a senior research fellow with the Longitudinal Employer Household Dynamics program at the Bureau of the Census. His recent research has exploited the newly created longitudinal establishment and firm level as well as matched employer-employee data that have been developed in the United States and around the world. This research centers on the process of reallocation and restructuring in developed, emerging, and transition economies and their connection to cyclical fluctuations and productivity growth. He is also affiliated with the Institute for the Study of Labor (IZA).

**Pierella Paci** is currently leading the Employment and Migration program of the Poverty Reduction and Economic Management (PREM) network at the World Bank. She has worked extensively in the areas of labor markets, poverty, income distribution, gender, and social policy and before joining the World Bank taught Labor Economics, Econometrics, Microeconomics, and Public Economics. She has a *laurea* degree in Economics from the University of Rome (Italy), an M.Sc. in Public Economics from the University of York, and a Ph.D. in Economics from the University of Manchester.

**Samir Radwan** is executive director of the Egyptian Competitiveness Council (ENCC) and specializes in employment policies, labor markets, industrial policies, and poverty in developing countries. He obtained his B.Sc. in Economics at the University of Cairo and his Ph.D. from the University of London. He was a lecturer in Economics at Cairo University, the University of Oxford, and the American University in Cairo. He worked with the International Labour Organization (ILO), and more recently he was managing director of the Economic Research Forum. He gave advice to numerous organizations (UNDP, World Bank, UN Food and Agricultural Organization, IFAD, OECD, Arab Labor Organization) and was a member of the Bruntland Commission. He was also an adviser to the Prime Minister of Egypt. He has published extensively on human resources development, labor markets, rural development, industrialization, and African and Arab economies.

**Justin Sandefur** is a doctoral candidate in the Department of Economics at Oxford University, affiliated with the Centre for the Study of African Economies (CSAE). His research to date has focused primarily on labor market dynamics and firm growth in Ghana and Tanzania, and increasingly on the evaluation of aid interventions.

**Pieter Serneels** is an economist at the World Bank. He has done extensive work on issues related to labor, poverty, and service delivery in low-income countries. He has held posts at the University of Oxford, the University of Copenhagen, and the ILO and has given advice to governments in developing countries. He holds an M.Sc. in Economics from Warwick University and a Ph.D. in Economics from the University of Oxford. He has published in peer-reviewed journals and contributed to books.

**Francis Teal** is currently director of the ESRC-funded Global Poverty Research Group (GPRG) and a deputy director of the Centre for the

Study of African Economies (CSAE) at Oxford University. Before joining the Centre he held positions in Tanzania at the Tanzania Investment Bank; at the School of Oriental and African Studies, University of London; and in Australia at the Australian National University. He has worked on a wide range of trade and development policy issues and has published in scholarly journals. He is currently working on projects studying the evolution of firms in Africa and links between firm growth and labor market outcomes.

**Christopher Woodruff** is an associate professor of economics at the Graduate School of International Relations and Pacific Studies at the University of California San Diego. He is an expert on small and medium-size enterprises in developing and transition economies. Woodruff's research has examined how firms do business with one another in environments in which inadequate legal systems make formal contracting difficult and the importance of access to finance. Geographically, his research spans a broad area of the developing world—Mexico, Vietnam, Sri Lanka, and Eastern Europe. His research has been published in the *American Economic Review; Quarterly Journal of Economics; Journal of Law, Economics and Organizations; Journal of Public Economics*, and other scholarly journals.

# Acronyms and Abbreviations

| | |
|---|---|
| ADB | Asian Development Bank |
| ENAMIN | National Survey of Microenterprises (Mexico) |
| ENEU | Mexican Urban Employment Survey |
| GCC | Gulf Cooperation Council |
| GDP | gross domestic product |
| HDNSP | Human Development Network, Social Protection Unit, World Bank |
| IADB | Inter-American Development Bank |
| ILO | International Labour Organization |
| LBD | longitudinal business database |
| LE | Egyptian pound (currency; local abbreviation) |
| LIC | low-income country |
| MENA | Middle East and North Africa |
| OECD | Organisation for Economic Co-operation and Development |
| PRMPR | Poverty Reduction and Development Effectiveness Department, World Bank |

# CHAPTER 1

# Introduction

## Pierella Paci and Pieter Serneels

### The Rationale for This Volume

How economic growth translates into poverty reduction differs across countries and varies over time. A key factor in this process is the way in which the benefits of growth are distributed across different income groups (Eastwood and Lipton 2000; Kakwani, Neri, and Son 2004). It is also acknowledged that the distribution of these benefits is highly associated with the quantity and quality of the new jobs created and with the barriers that prevent the poor from accessing existing opportunities. That is not surprising, as worldwide the vast majority of people, especially the poor, depend on their labor as the primary source of income. However, the understanding of the links among growth, employment, and poverty reduction remains limited.

This volume is intended to make an initial contribution to gaining a better understanding of these issues and to encourage further work in this area. The focus is on labor market mobility as engine of growth and as a powerful transmission mechanism between growth and poverty reduction. This introductory chapter begins by reviewing the literature on labor markets, growth, and poverty and highlights the importance of mobility for labor market efficiency. It is well known that this literature is limited in quantity and scope and that this is primarily the result of the lack of a unifying framework. In order to guide future work, we set out the contours for such a framework.

### Employment and Mobility as Engine of Shared Growth

Most people who move out of poverty do so by increasing their earnings from work. At the household level there are essentially three ways in which earnings from work can be increased: (i) by working more hours; (ii) by increasing the effort per hour worked—that is, increasing labor productivity in order to increase hourly earnings; and (iii) by moving to a job that gives higher returns for a given level of productivity. Existing analytical work focuses on the first mechanism, employment generation, as a way to reduce poverty, and less attention is paid to improving labor productivity or access to better-paid jobs as a way to reduce poverty.[1]

However, in low-income countries (LICs) poverty is less likely to be the consequence of lack of employment than of low productivity and limited access to well-paid jobs. This is underscored by the large number of working poor. A recent report by the International Labour Organization (ILO) estimates that there are roughly seven times as many working poor worldwide as there are unemployed (ILO 2007): more than 500 million people, or 18 percent of the global work force. And although their number has fallen, this decline has been driven essentially by developments in China, South Asia, and middle-income countries, while low-income countries have seen an *increase* in the number of working poor.[2]

Employment generation remains, of course, an important target for economic policy, as the creation of additional employment opportunities is, among other things, essential to absorb the fast growing population of LICs. However, creating more jobs is *not enough*, as the majority of the population in LICs works in small-scale enterprises that generate low income, and this is likely to persist in the near future. For these workers, the objective is to increase their earnings primarily by improving productivity in the same job—earnings mobility—or by improving their chances to move to employment that offers higher returns, that is, occupational mobility. This book focuses on these two issues, addressing questions like: Are people mobile across jobs, firms, or sectors? Do they face barriers to mobility, and what are these barriers? If people do not move across sectors, does it mean they are "stuck" in certain types of jobs? Does this prevent them from increasing their productivity and improving their earnings in these types of jobs? The chapters that follow provide only partial answers, but they underline that focusing on mobility—or the lack thereof—is the way forward to understanding the role of labor markets for growth and poverty reduction.

The idea that labor mobility is of central importance in understanding the functioning of the economy is not new.[3] However, empirical analysis of labor mobility and its impact on development remains limited, especially for LICs. Shortage of adequate data, especially panel data, is often indicated as the main reason for this scarcity, but the last decade has seen a substantial increase in data availability in LICs. So lack of data is rapidly becoming less of a constraint, and a growing volume of the available information remains considerably underexploited in the absence of a widely accepted unifying framework and of empirically testable hypotheses.[4]

For years, views on how best to model labor markets in LICs have been highly polarized. The supporters of traditional neoclassical theory saw the labor market as a unified, perfectly competitive entity, a view deeply questioned by others who believed the reality of developing countries to be better described by a framework allowing for a number of different labor markets operating under different market conditions and with different degrees of interaction.

Although this divergence of views encouraged further work in the 1970s, it seems to have stifled the debate in the 1980s and 1990s. Fortunately, however, the growing recognition of the role of institutions and regulations seems to have increased the awareness that there are major rigidities in almost all labor markets, and this has created a new willingness to discuss the coexistence of different labor markets.[5] When putting together different strands of the recent literature, a new framework seems to be emerging. However, so far the debate has concentrated mostly on whether policy interventions should focus on increasing earnings in the sectors in which the poor are concentrated (such as agriculture), or whether they should target sectors in which the poor are not well represented, so that more of them can be drawn into the higher-earning sectors in response to increased demand for labor (Fields 2006). Very little attention has been devoted to policies designed to remove the existing barriers to low-paid workers accessing higher-paying sectors.

This volume is intended to increase awareness of the potential role of mobility for shared growth and of the multifaceted aspects of this process by presenting selected papers on issues at the frontier of labor economics. Each chapter gives a different view on the same underlying puzzle: how important is mobility in the labor market for generating growth and moving out of poverty? The puzzle is approached in different ways, and some of the papers represent the first application of innovative methodologies to LICs.

## The Links Among Employment, Growth, and Poverty: A Brief Overview of Existing Work

The literature on the links between employment, growth, and poverty can be divided into two quite separate strands. The first focuses on the employment-growth link—including analysis of the impact of labor regulations. The other focuses more on the relationships among employment outcomes, poverty, and pro-poor growth.

### Links between Labor Market and Growth

Although generalized agreement on the importance of labor market structure and outcomes for growth exists, analytical work on the relationship remains limited. The empirical growth literature of the past 15 years, for example, has paid little attention to the role of labor markets in economic performance. Barro (1991) explains the variation in long-run growth rates across countries as a function of their initial level of development, investment in physical and human capital, and the degree of political stability. Later models built on a variety of extensions, as reviewed by Sala-i-Martin (1997),[6] but none of these—including state-of-the-art references on endogenous growth such as Aghion and Howitt (1998)—explicitly model the labor market. Similarly, the effect of economic performance on earnings and working conditions has remained largely unaddressed, as illustrated by Rama and Artecona (2002).

Furthermore, the existing literature on this issue is heavily biased toward high-income countries and has for the most part neglected developing and transition economies. That has been changing over the past five years, and there is now a small body of work on labor and growth in LICs, with most of it focusing on institutions and regulations. Forteza and Rama (2001), for instance, find that countries with relatively rigid labor markets experience deeper recessions before adjustment and slower recoveries afterward. They find that minimum wages and mandatory benefits do not hurt growth but that the relative size of organized labor (in government and elsewhere) does. Calderon and Chong (2005), using a Barro-style model, find that both minimum wages and unionization affect growth negatively and argue that reducing the existing labor regulations may increase growth potentials. Cukierman, Rama, and Van Ours (2001) find a nonlinear relationship between minimum wages and growth: raising a low minimum wage stimulates growth, but the impact is negligible when the minimum wage is higher. Heckman and Pages (2000), using data for Latin America and Europe, illustrate the importance of other labor market institutions such as job security and mandated benefits. They find them to widen wage inequality, reduce employment, and have a potential negative effect on growth prospects.

The difficulty with evaluating the impact of regulations, however, is that they change only rarely over time, so that it is difficult to set up an adequate counterfactual. This makes analysis of intercountry differences in regulations particularly valuable. Two papers exploit the legal adaptations of national laws by individual states in India to address this issue. Besley and Burgess (2004) find that those states that amended the Industrial Relation Disputes Act in a pro-worker direction have lower output, employment, investment, and productivity in formal manufacturing, whereas output in informal manufacturing increased. Ahsan and Pages (2005), extending this study, find that amendments that increased the stringency of the procedures for resolving labor disputes and changing job security regulations hurt registered workers and affect labor-intensive industries in particular. They also find that the use of contract labor increases but that this does not compensate for the adverse effects of labor laws on employment. Summarizing the research on Latin America and the Caribbean, Arias et al. (2005) provide a more general picture, arguing that existing regulations may be reducing job turnover and job creation, limiting the efficiency of the economy to adapt to change. Micco and Pages (2006), using a large sample of Latin American and European countries, make a similar case and argue that more stringent legislation slows down job turnover, which affects in particular output in sectors that are intrinsically more volatile.

### Links between Employment Outcomes and Poverty

The most comprehensive analysis on the link between employment outcomes and poverty is a collection of 14 case studies carried out by the World Bank (2006a) that finds that highly regulated labor markets restrict participation of the poor in economic growth. The study also identifies the ability to migrate as an important factor enabling the poor to benefit from growth. Using country-level data, Lustig and McLeod (1996) conclude that minimum wages do not reduce poverty in developing countries and that the evidence for richer countries is inconclusive. Besley and Burgess (2004) find that pro-worker labor regulation coincides with an increase in urban poverty in India, although it is unclear in which direction the relationship goes and how far regulation reflects a poor labor relations climate. Many of the other contributions remain descriptive or focus on specific effects, providing limited insights into the wider functioning of the labor market or the economy-wide effects.[7]

A small separate body of work focuses on the impact of employment generation on pro-poor growth. Among them, the World Bank (2005) concludes that access to nonfarm rural employment and informal urban employment facilitates participation of the poor in the growth process. Kakwani, Neri, and Son (2004) decompose the sources of pro-poor growth in Brazil and identify improved productivity as the main engine of labor income growth, whereas social security benefits and cash transfers are the main sources of growth in nonlabor income. By way of contrast, using data for five Asian countries, Osmani (2005) concludes that poverty reduction was more significant in those countries in which growth translated into both more and better employment.[8]

### A Largely Unexplored Issue

The existing work on growth and poverty leaves the role of employment in the transmission process largely unexplored.[9] At the same time, there is a rich tradition of labor market analysis in developing countries that takes a mainly microeconomic approach and covers a wide range of topics. Themes as diverse as returns to education (Bigsten et al. 2000), female labor supply (Psacharopoulos and Tzannatos 1989), off-farm work (Lanjouw and Lanjouw 1995; Haggblade et al. 1989), the role of nutrition (Strauss and Thomas 1998), migration (Stark 1990), and the evaluation of labor programs (Ravallion 1999) have been studied.

Overall this work has not received the attention that it deserves because it has remained largely outside mainstream labor economics, as it frequently relies on a multisector or segmented market models.[10] Although this model was popular among mainstream economists in the late 1960s and early 1970s, it was subsequently neglected after two influential negative reviews (see Wachter 1974 and Cain 1976) heavily criticized the apparent lack of a solid theoretical model behind the interesting working hypothesis. However, the rise of efficiency wage theory, which provided a powerful explanation of why high wages may be persistent in one sector but not necessarily in another, brought about a renewed interest in segmented markets and led to empirical testing. Although segmentation is very hard to prove formally,[11] most economists now agree that segmented labor market models have much to offer and that their explanatory power is too strong for them to be neglected altogether.[12] This is also acknowledged by policy makers and advisors, as the good jobs-bad jobs dichotomy is now widely being used by national and international policy makers.[13]

## Toward an Integrated Framework and the Role of Labor Mobility

Despite this renewed interest, a unifying framework that integrates the different theoretical approaches and fully analyzes the role of employment as a transmission factor between growth and poverty reduction is still missing. However, some promising attempts are emerging, including two lines of contemporary work that focus on labor market mobility as a central element of a growth model.

The starting point of the first school of thought builds on the theory of structural change as set out by Chenery and Syrquin (1975) and extended by Chenery, Robinson, and Syrquin (1986).[14] It sees the economy as consisting of a number of different sectors and economic growth as being to a large extent affected and driven by the relative size and productivity of these sectors. The typical approach is then to integrate this notion of segmentation and structural change dynamics in a simple growth regression (see, for example, Caselli and Coleman 2001; Lucas 2004; Ngai and Pissarides 2004; and Robertson 1999). The theory behind the second approach is that of creative destruction, which argues that the birth and death of firms—and thus jobs—is a natural process and that a certain amount of churning is needed to generate economic growth (see Schumpeter and Opie 1961). This work analyzes flows of workers and jobs to understand the movements underlying the growth process and the barriers to growth, including the mismatches that occur in the labor market (see, for example, Davis et al. 2006).[15]

The common assumptions underlying both schools of thought are that (i) labor mobility plays a key role in the growth process and in the way its benefits are shared across individuals; and (ii) the prevailing labor market institutions and regulations affect the degree of mobility. In many ways the two approaches are complementary. Whereas the first typically uses cross-country evidence, the latter uses microdata on firms and workers. The way forward then is to integrate these two approaches and create a new framework that allows the relationship between labor mobility and growth, at both the micro- and macroeconomic levels, to be analyzed. Current work in this direction suggests indeed that this will be a fruitful approach. Temple and Woessman (2004), using cross-country data, find, for example, that the (successful) reallocation of labor across sectors explains a substantial fraction of international variation in total factor productivity, while Satchi and Temple (2006) find evidence that the efficiency of matches can have a significant impact on output.[16] Other work illustrates that this framework also makes it possible to look at the links with poverty. Loayza and Raddatz (2006), for example, show that the sector composition of growth matters for poverty reduction, with unskilled labor-intensive sectors making the largest contributions. Satchi and Temple (2006) also analyze the link with poverty; they find that the efficiency of the matching process affects the income from labor and thus poverty.

While this work illustrates the strong appeal of an integrated framework with labor mobility at its core, it also indicates that more work is needed to enrich our basic understanding. In response to this need the Poverty Reduction and Development Effectiveness Department (PRMPR) of the World Bank has begun a multiyear work program in this area. This volume is one of the first outputs of this program. It brings together five very different papers that share a microeconomic perspective and the common focus on the role of labor mobility for growth and poverty reduction.

## Five Topics at the Frontier

The volume covers five topics: (i) multisector labor markets, (ii) informality, (iii) self-employment, (iv) mobility and earnings, and (v) the role of firm dynamics.

Underlying the volume is the notion that the labor market in developing countries is not homogeneous. On the contrary, it is highly fragmented, with many different segments offering employment opportunities that differ considerably in their characteristics and in the rewards they generate. Thus the volume begins with Gary Fields setting out the concept of *multisector labor market* (chapter 2), with different segments offering qualitatively distinct types of employment. The higher earnings segment(s) is (are) restricted in the sense that not everyone who wants a good job obtains one. Workers with similar characteristics are thus paid a different wage depending on the sector in which they work.[17]

Traditionally, the theoretical literature has focused on dualism, and empirical analysis has for the most compared two sectors—that is, urban versus rural, formal versus informal, industry versus agriculture, assuming that the former usually offers better returns to labor than the latter for identical productivity. But evidence shows that there is substantial heterogeneity and limited mobility *within* each sector. For example, the urban sector is subdivided into a formal and an informal segment, and mobility between the two is often limited; off-farm work is often more rewarding than farm work but not accessible to everyone; and some industrial jobs are more attractive than others but also more difficult to get. It is therefore important to consider a higher degree of segmentation. A traditional approach has been to consider at least three sectors: the rural or agricultural sector, the urban formal sector, and the urban informal sector. For some countries, a still higher degree of segmentation is warranted, and it is necessary to make a distinction within the informal sector between an upper tier, which contains dynamic entrepreneurs that earn well, and a lower tier composed mostly of household businesses that are part of a survival economy. For others, an important distinction is between public and private employment.

However, to understand fully the working of the multisector labor market, two additional dimensions have to be understood: the different mechanism by which wages are set within each sector and the way in which the sectors are linked. As Fields points out, wages may be set by market forces, or they may be set above market clearing levels because of efficiency wage considerations, institutional factors, or worker-side considerations like unions. Even when market forces are at play the market is rarely competitive, and the remuneration may differ from the individual's value product—that is, under labor market monopsony. More importantly, the links between the different segments depend largely on the extent and nature of mobility between the sectors, or whether those not employed in a good job take up a bad job or stay unemployed. As Fields confirms, consensus that the multisegmented labor market model is a fair reflection of the reality in developing countries has been growing among both academics and policy makers. His contribution on multisectoral labor markets provides a practical starting point for policy makers on how to go beyond the single labor market approach and beyond dualism in country-level work. An additional benefit of the multisector model is that it can be adapted to the local reality, allowing policy makers to move away from the "one size fits all" approach and to address questions in a tailor-made fashion.

In chapter 3, Samir Radwan applies the multisector model to the Middle East and North Africa (MENA) region. Although in this region the informal sector was initially marginal in size and was perceived as a transition status for those waiting for a good (formal) job, its share in employment has dramatically grown over the past three decades, and it appears to be increasingly seen as a permanent state of employment. Informal nonagricultural employment is for the most part, but not exclusively, associated with low pay and poor working conditions, and mobility from the informal to the formal sector remains limited. However, evidence is growing that the informal sector may have the potential to enhance both the quality and the quantity of the employment opportunities it offers. Thus the crucial policy question is how to improve the quality of jobs in this kind of setting.

To understand how this can be done succesfully, Radwan carries out a deeper analysis of the structure of the economy and the nature of the informal sector, distinguishing three types of economies in the region: oil economies or Gulf Cooperation Council (GCC) countries; economies that have a labor surplus and that have diversified their economic activities, like Egypt, Jordan, Morocco, and Tunisia; and marginalized economies like Sudan, Yemen, and Somalia. The characteristics and causes of poor employment opportunities are different for the different types of economies.

In the GCC *countries* bad jobs are mostly taken up by foreign workers who do not enjoy the same privileges as nationals, and they exist almost exclusively because of regulation. Improving the quality of these jobs would require a shift in national migration policies, which is politically difficult to implement. In the *marginalized economies*, the constraints lie outside the labor market, as the main problem here is a lack of overall growth, often attributable to weak economic policies, and informal work is mostly a survival strategy for the poor. For the *labor surplus economies* the multisector model provides a useful framework, as a key constraint to improve the employment opportunities is the lack of mobility between the informal and formal sectors. High transaction costs, mostly resulting from complex regulations, keep firms small and informal, prohibiting entrepreneurs in the informal sector from growing and becoming formal. In Egypt, for example, where the informal sector represents about 55 percent of nonagriculture employment, informal entrepreneurs are estimated to own about US$240 billion, or two and a half times GDP, in dead capital, as argued in a study by Hemando de Soto. Simplifying regulations would reduce transaction costs and release this capital. But will this process of formalization lead to sustainable growth and create enough good jobs in the region to absorb the growing active population? Or are more large-scale investors needed? Whether the self-employed can raise their income and be an engine of growth is a question that is investigated in more depth in chapter 4.

An alternative and often used characterization of a segmented labor market is based on employment status, that is, whether the individual is a wage worker, self-employed, or an unpaid family member.[18] This approach is used in chapters 4 and 5. Whether employment status offers an accurate description of the different segments in the labor market is debatable. Evidence suggests that heterogeneity among the self-employed is often large and that self-employment may be a well-paid choice for some. As with the debate on informality, using the multisector model offers a way out, as one can distinguish between upper- and lower-tier self-employment as two separate segments. The key question is then whether there is mobility within this sector, that is, whether the self-employed can move easily from the lower to the upper tier (and from self-employment into wage employment). If this is the case, given that in low-income countries the self-employed often represent the largest sector of the economy, self-employment can be the engine of growth.

In chapter 4, Chris Woodruff uses data for Mexico to investigate this hypothesis. A novelty of this work is that it offers a convincing way to identify the heterogeneity among the self-employed by distinguishing between those who work for their own account or use only family labor on the one hand—these represent the vast majority—and those who hire paid workers from outside the family on the other hand. As expected, he finds large differences in earnings and characteristics between the two groups of workers: those employing outsiders earn more, have higher levels of education, are more likely to come from families of business owners, and have parents with higher income and higher education levels. Since these characteristics are already determined when someone enters the labor market, Woodruff argues, it is unlikely that the self-employed in the lower tier, which are the majority of self-employed, will move upward to the higher tier.

Woodruff also finds that the returns to capital among the self-employed, including microentrepreneurs, are high. This suggests that capital injections can increase the returns to labor in this sector and that access to capital is a potential constraint to upward mobility. Thus policies designed to weaken existing credit constraints by, for example, improving access to microfinance, are highlighted as potentially effective ways of improving the quality of employment opportunities and lifting some people out of poverty. However, the increase in the returns to labor is unlikely to be large enough to spur growth. Thus the Mexican evidence suggests that self-employment is unlikely to provide an effective source of sustained job creation and growth.

Chapter 5 continues in a similar vein by investigating the relative magnitude of the impact of mobility across and within employment status on labor income in three Sub-Saharan African countries: Ethiopia,

Ghana, and Tanzania. Using unique panel data, the authors compare the determinants of earnings of workers in the formal sector and the self-employed. They find their lifecycle earnings profile to be remarkably similar when comparing workers in firms of the same size, implying that differences in the return to labor have more to do with the size of the firm than with employment status as such. This result confirms findings from other countries in Africa and is consistent with Woodruff's finding in chapter 4 that the self-employed who employ nonfamily members—who typically tend to have a larger business—have higher returns. The authors also find that mobility across sectors (defined in terms of employment status) appears to be limited, suggesting that the labor market may indeed be segmented along employment status. Combined, these findings suggest that increases in labor income are, for the most part associated with higher earnings in existing jobs rather than with movements to better-paid sectors.

Chapters 4 and 5 underline the importance of firm characteristics for segmentation but either restrict the analysis to the self-employed (Chapter 4) or rely on individual worker data (chapter 5). Chapter 6 provides a complementary approach by using firm-level data. As firm data are still a rare luxury in many developing countries, this chapter relies mostly on data from advanced, emerging, and transition economies and aims to illustrate the rich insights that can be generated from analyzing such data. While mobility remains the underlying issue of relevance, the focus here is on job flows, or how employment opportunities change in one sector relative to another as a result of firm dynamics that bring about job creation and destruction. The economy is seen as in a constant flux as firms are born, expand, contract, and die, creating and destroying jobs in the process. From an economy-wide perspective, this process of creative destruction is important for growth, as the entry and expansion of the more productive firms combined with the exit and contraction of the less productive ones constitute an important engine of productivity increases. John Haltiwanger provides a useful method to measure job flows based on the concepts of *net growth rate in jobs* and *rate of job allocation*. The former is the difference between job creation and job destruction and the latter the sum of job creation and job destruction. These measures serve as a starting point to assess job flows and the allocative efficiency of an economy.

Applying these measures to the data, some stylized facts emerge. Job flows are high everywhere, and entry and exit of businesses play an important role in economic development. However, the magnitude of the flows varies significantly across industrial sectors and the size of firms, while the role of institutions is unclear. The first finding suggests that the relative differences in productivity between sectors—which affect growth according to the structural change literature—are related to the differences in job flows in these sectors. The importance of firm size suggests that large firms do not just offer better paid jobs, as seen in chapter 5, but also provide more stability. An additional interesting finding is that young firms experience more volatile growth and are key for job and productivity growth in the United States but not in emerging and transition countries.

## Summary and Conclusion

This chapter argues that labor market mobility is a central, but often neglected, link between growth and poverty reduction. Especially in low-income countries, poverty is associated with low-pay employment rather than with "being without work." The large number of working poor have two possible ways of increasing their earnings: by becoming more productive (income mobility) or by getting access to a better paid job (job mobility). However, the current mindset still puts too much emphasis on job creation and the quantity of work, and not enough on its quality and on the degree of mobility between jobs of different quality.

One of the reasons for this is the lack of a unifying framework that clearly identifies the potential role of mobility in an analytically sound and empirically testable way. The views on how best to model labor markets, especially in LICs, have been highly polarized between those who believe in a single, perfectly competitive market and defendants of segmented labor market models. However, increased attention to the role of institutions and regulations seems to have raised the awareness that most labor markets have important rigidities, and this has created a new openness for discussion. The central notion of the unified framework we propose is that growth is driven by the relative size and productivity in different sectors and that labor mobility is needed to spur growth.[19] Each of the papers in this volume addresses a specific topic related to labor mobility. In chapter 2 Gary Fields discusses why multisector labor markets provide a good starting point. Samir Radwan, in chapter 3, investigates the role of the informal sector, focusing on the MENA Region; Chris Woodruff looks at self-employment in chapter 4, using data from Mexico. Chapter 5 compares mobility within and between sectors in three African countries; and chapter 6 takes the perspective of the labor demand side, focusing on job flows in a sample of advanced, emerging, and transition countries.

Much work remains to be done, and these papers point out some ways forward. They underline the fact that a better understanding of existing barriers to labor mobility is crucial to enhance the potential for shared growth and for a more effective working of the transmission channels between growth and poverty reduction. The current PREM program on *Employment and Shared Growth* is defined to address these issues more deeply.

## Notes

1. Both Islam (2004) and Osmani (2005), for example, find that when employment expands with growth, poverty tends to decline.

2. The decline in working poor is estimated at 5 percent over the last 8 years, but the working poor in low-income countries other than India and China, now represent 95 percent of those employed, compared to 88 percent before.

3. For an early contribution, see for example Lewis (1954).

4. A recent study on labor diagnostics and their availability for Sub-Saharan Africa suggests that existing data are underexploited (see World Bank PREMPR 2007).

5. Two important contributions in this area have been Nickell (1996), who provides empirical evidence on the role of institutions in OECD, and Saint Paul (1996), who provides a theoretical treatment of the coexistence of good and bad jobs.

6. He identifies 63 different variables that have been used, from fiscal policy, monetary policy, trade openness, financial development, to social capital, geography, and religious background.

7. See, for example, Lanjouw (2001) and Ravallion and Huppi (1990).

8. A separate strand of literature focuses on the employment elasticity of growth. As Fields argues in the next chapter, this concept has problems. And from an empirical perspective, the results are not robust. Islam (2004) uses data for 23 developing countries to analyze whether the employment intensity of growth in manufacturing contributes to explaining poverty reduction, but finds that results are not robust to the inclusion of per capita GDP growth. Rao et al. (2004) find that the significance of output per worker in explaining poverty reduction was not robust to the inclusion of log of GDP per capita.

9. Still another strand of the literature that analyzes the growth elasticity of poverty (as opposed to the levels of poverty discussed above) also pays very limited attention to labor markets, although a wide variety of other factors is considered (see, for example, Bourguignon 2002; Chen and Ravillion 2004; Dollar and Kraay 2002; Kraay 2006; Ravallion 2005; and Ravillion and Datt 2001). A notable exception is Loayza and Raddatz (2006), who consider the

growth impact in unskilled-labor-intensive sectors and find that growth in these sectors raised the wage of unskilled labor and thus helped to explain the differences in the growth elasticity of poverty.

10. Segmented labor market theory distinguishes itself from the more classical labor theory by stressing the variation in job characteristics, instead of individual characteristics.

11. There is no convincing empirical method of testing the segmented versus the competitive labor market hypothesis because unobserved individual characteristics may drive self-selection. The discussion on segmentation spans a long period. Perhaps initiated by Lewis (1954), and made more explicit by Doeringer and Piore (1970), the discussion was continued by Dickens and Lang (1985), Heckman and Sedlacek (1985), Heckman and Hotz (1985), Dickens and Lang (1987), and Magnac (1991).

12. Labor market segmentation is now part of the standard labor economic textbooks (see, for example, Borjas 1996; Bosworth et al. 1996; and Layard, Nickel, and Jackson 1991). The main reason is that it offers a better explanation for some empirical observations than the competitive model. An often-quoted example is the persistent existence of intra-industry wage differentials for observationally equivalent workers (Katz and Summers 1988). For other contributions, see Dickens and Lang (1988) and Esfahani and Salehi-Isfahani (1989).

13. It is used by the World Bank, the ILO, the Inter-American Development Bank, and the Asian Development Bank, among others, as illustrated by Fields in chapter 2.

14. Which can be traced back further to dual economy models, particularly familiar to development economists through the work of Lewis (1954).

15. By considering different types of jobs (and workers), this approach also allows explicitly to revisit questions formerly addressed under the label of "segmentation."

16. See also Landon-Lane and Robertson (2003), Poirson (2000, 2001), and Paci and Pigliary (1999), who take a similar approach.

17. This is the classic definition of segmentation. As pointed out above, formal testing of segmentation is difficult, as unobserved characteristics may explain part of the difference in earnings.

18. "Unpaid family worker" is the term used for family members working in a household enterprise and not receiving cash payment.

19. Since from a worker's perspective job instability often implies adverse consequences, this has given rise to labor regulations and institutions that protect workers. At the same time, job flows are important to keep an economy dynamic and growing. Therefore, good institutions are the ones that balance job flows and social protection, and bring about an optimal degree of mobility.

## Bibliography

Aghion, P., and P. Howitt. 1998. *Endogenous Growth Theory*, Cambridge and London: MIT Press.

Ahsan, A., and C. Pages. 2005. "Helping or Hurting Workers? Assessing the Effects of De Jure and De Facto Labor Regulations in India." Mimeo. World Bank.

Arellano, M., and S. Bond. 1991. "Some Tests of Specification for Panel Data: Monte Carlo Evidence and an Application to Employment Equations." *Review of Economic Studies* 58: 277–97.

Arias, O., A. Blom, M. Bosch, W. Cunningham, A. Fiszbein, A. G. López, W. Maloney, J. Saavedra, C. Sánchez-Páramo, M. Santamaría, L. Siga. 2005. "Pending Issues in Protection, Productivity Growth, and Poverty Reduction." Policy research working paper. World Bank, Washington, DC.

Barro, R. 1991. "Economic Growth in a Cross Section of Countries." *Quarterly Journal of Economics* 106 (2): 407–43.

Bentolila, S., and G. de Saint-Paul. 1992. "Model of Labour Demand with Linear Adjustment Costs." Discussion Paper Series No. 690, 1–34. Centre for Economic Policy Research, London.

Bernal, R., and M. Cárdenas. 2003. "Determinants of Labor Demand in Colombia: 1976–1996." Working Paper Series No. 10077, 1–51. NBER (National Bureau of Economic Research), Cambridge, MA.

Besley, T., and R. Burgess. 2004. "Can Labor Regulation Hinder Economic Performance? Evidence from India." *Quarterly Journal of Economics* 119 (1): 91–134.

Besley, T., and L. J. Cord. 2007. *Delivering on the Promise of Pro-Poor Growth. Insights and Lessons from Country Experiences*. Hampshire, England: Palgrave Macmillan; Washington, DC: World Bank.

Bigsten, A., A. I. Isaksson, M. Söderbom, P. Collier, A. G. Zeufack, S. Dercon, M. Fafchamps, J. Gunning, F. Teal, S. Appleton, B. P. Gauthier, A. D. Oduro, R. Oostendorp, C. A. Pattillo. 2000. "Rates of Return on Physical and Human Capital in Africa's Manufacturing Sector." *Economic Development and Cultural Change* 48 (4): 801–27.

Borjas, G. J. 1996. *Labor Economics*. New York: McGraw-Hill.

Boserup, E. 1981. *Population and Technological Change*. Chicago, IL: University of Chicago Press.

Bosworth, D., P. Dawkins, T. Stromback. 1996. *The Economics of the Labor Market*. Essex, England: Addison Wesley Longman, Ltd.

Bourguignon, F. 2002. "The Growth Elasticity of Poverty Reduction: Explaining Heterogeneity Across Countries and Time Periods." DELTA working paper. DELTA, http://www.delta.ens.fr/

Cain, G. G. 1976. "The Challenge of the Segmented Labor Market Theories to Orthodox Theory: A Survey." *Journal of Economic Literature* 14: 1215–57.

Calderon, C., and A. Chong. 2005. "Are Labor Market Regulations an Obstacle for Long-Term Growth?" In *Labor Markets and Institutions*, ed. J. E. Restrepo and A. Tokman. Santiago, Chile: Central Bank of Chile.

Cardenas, M., and C. Gutiérrez. 1996. "Impacto de las reformas estructurales sobre la efficiencia y la equidad: la experiencia Colombiana en los 90." *Coyuntura Economica* XXVI (4).

Caselli, F., and W. J. Coleman II. 2001. "The U.S. Structural Transformation and Regional Convergence: A Reinterpretation." *Journal of Political Economy* 109 (3): 584–616.

Chen, S., and M. Ravallion. 2004. "How Have the World's Poorest Fared Since the Early 1980s?" *World Bank Research Observer* 19 (2): 141–69.

Chenery, H. B., S. Robinson, and M. Syrquin. 1986. *Industrialization and Growth: A Comparative Study*. New York: Oxford University Press for the World Bank.

Chenery, H. B., and M. Syrquin. 1975. *Patterns of Development, 1950–1970*. London: Oxford University Press for the World Bank.

Cukierman, A., M. Rama, and J. Van Ours. 2001. "Long-Run Growth, the Minimum Wage and Other Labor Market Institutions. Preliminary Notes." Mimeo. http://www.tau.ac.il/~alexcuk/pdf/GrowthB.pdf

Davis, S. J., R. J. Faberman, J. C. Haltiwanger. 2006. "The Flow Approach to Labor Markets: New Data Sources and Micro-Macro Links." *Journal of Economic Perspectives* 20 (3): 3–26.

Deaton, A. 2005. "Measuring Poverty in a Growing World (or Measuring Growth in a Poor World)." *Review of Economics and Statistics* 87 (1): 1–25.

Dickens, W. T., and K. Lang. 1985. "Testing Dual Labor Market Theory: A Reconsideration of the Evidence." Working Paper Series No. 1670, 1–27. NBER, Cambridge, MA.

———. 1987. "Goodness of Fit Test of Dual Labor Market Theory." Working Paper Series No. 2350, 1–9. NBER, Cambridge, MA.

———. 1988. "Reemergence of Segmented Labor Market Theory." *American Economic Review, Papers and Proceedings* 78: 129–34.

Diewert, W. E. 1971. "An Application of Shepard Duality Theorem: A Generalized Production Function." *Journal of Political Economy* 79: 481–507.

Dollar, D., and A. Kraay. 2002. "Growth Is Good for the Poor." *Journal of Economic Growth* 7 (3): 195–225.

Dowrick, S., and N. Gemmel. 1991. "Industrialisation, Catching Up and Economic Growth: A Comparative Study Across the World's Capitalist Economies." *Economic Journal* 101 (405): 263–75.

Eastwood, Reduction and M. Lipton (2000), Pro-Poor Growth and Pro-Growth Poverty Reduction: Meaning, Evidence and Policy Implications, Asian Development Review, 2.

Esfahani, H. S., and D. Salehi-Isfahani. 1989. "Effort Observability and Worker Productivity: Towards an Explanation of Economic Dualism." *The Economic Journal* 99: 818–36.

Fields, G. 2006. "Employment in Low-Income Countries beyond Labor Market Segmentation?" Document prepared for the World Bank conference "Rethinking the Role of Jobs for Shared Growth," Washington, DC, June 19, 2006.

Forteza, A., and M. Rama. 2001. "Labor Market 'Rigidity' and the Success of Economic Reforms Across More than One Hundred Countries." Policy Research Working Paper 2521. World Bank, Washington, DC.

Goodman, L. 1960. "On the Exact Variance of Products." *Journal of the American Statistical Association* 55 (292): 708–13.

Haggblade, S., P. Hazell, J. Brown. 1989. "Farm-Nonfarm Linkages in Rural Sub-Saharan Africa." *World Development* 17: 1173–1201.

Hamermesh, D. S. 1986. "The Demand for Labor in the Long Run." In *Handbook of Labor Economics*, ed. O. Ashenfelter and R. Layard, I: 429–71. Amsterdam: Elsevier Science Publisher.

———. 1993. *Labor Demand*. Princeton, NJ: Princeton University Press.

Heckman, J. J., and V. J. Hotz. 1985. "Investigation of the Labor Market Earnings of Panamanian Males: Evaluating Sources of Inequality." Working Paper No. 8529C, 1–43. Centre for the Study of International Economic Relations, University of Western Ontario.

Heckman, J. J., and C. Pages. 2000. "The Cost of Job Security Regulation: Evidence from Latin American Labor Markets." Working Paper Series No. 7773, 1–38. NBER, Cambridge, MA.

Heckman, J. J., and G. Sedlacek. 1985. "Heterogeneity, Aggregation, and Market Wage Functions: An Empirical Model of Self-Selection in the Labor Market." *Journal of Political Economy* 93: 1077–125.

ILO. 2003. *Review of the Core Elements of the Global Employment Agenda*. Geneva, Switzerland: Committee on Employment and Social Policy Documents.

ILO. 2007. *Global employment Trends*. Geneva, Switzerland.

Islam, R. 2004. "The Nexus of Economic Growth, Employment and Poverty Reduction: An Empirical Analysis." Issues in Employment and Poverty Discussion Paper 14. ILO, New York.

Jackman, R., R. Layard, S. Savouri. 1991. "Mismatch: A Framework for Thought." In *Mismatch and Labour Mobility*, ed. F. Padoa Schioppa, 44–104. Cambridge, England: Cambridge University Press.

Kakwani, N., S. Khandker, and H. Son. 2004. "Pro-Poor Growth: Concepts and Measurement with Country Case Studies." Working paper. UNDP International Poverty Center, Brazil.

Kakwani, N., M. Neri, H. Son. 2004. "Linkages between Pro-Poor Growth, Social Programmes and Labour Market: The Recent Brazilian Experience." Working Paper. UNDP International Poverty Center, Brazil.

Katz, L. F., and K. M. Murphy. 1991. "Changes in Relative Wages, 1963–1987: Supply and Demand Factors." Working Paper Series No. 3927. NBER, Cambridge, MA.

Katz, L. F., and L. H. Summers. 1988. "Can Inter-Industry Wage Differentials Justify Strategic Trade Policy?" Working Paper Series No. 2739. NBER, Cambridge, MA.

Kraay, A. 2006. "When Is Growth Pro-Poor? Evidence from a Panel of Countries." *Journal of Development Economics* 80 (1): 198–227.

Landon-Lane, J., and P. E. Robertson. 2003. "Accumulation and Productivity Growth in Industrializing Economies." Manuscript. University of New South Wales, Australia.

Lanjouw, P. 2001. "Nonfarm Employment and Poverty in Rural El Salvador." *World Development* 29 (3): 529–47.

Lanjouw, P., and J. O. Lanjouw. 1995. *Rural Nonfarm Employment: A Survey*. Washington, DC: World Bank Office of the Vice President, Development Economics.

Layard, P. R. G., S. J. Nickell, R. Jackson 1991. *Unemployment: Macroeconomic Performance and the Labour Market*. Oxford & New York: Oxford University Press.

Lewis, W. A. 1954. "Economic Development with Unlimited Supplies of Labour." In *The Manchester School* 22: 139–91.

Loayza, N., and C. Raddatz. 2006. "The Composition of Growth Matters for Poverty Alleviation." Mimeo. http://www-wds.worldbank.org/servlet/ WDS ContentServer/WDSP/IB/2006/12/05/000016406_20061205152514/Rend ered/PDF/wps4077.pdf

Lucas, R. E. 2004. "Life Earnings and Rural-Urban Migration." *Journal of Political Economy* 112 (1, part 2, supplement): S29–S59.

Lucas, S., and P. Timmer. 2005. "Connecting the Poor to Economic Growth: Eight Key Questions." Working Briefs. Center for Global Development, Washington, DC.

Lustig, N., and D. McLeod. 1996. "Minimum Wages and Poverty in Developing Countries: Some Empirical Evidence." Brookings Discussion Papers in International Economics No. 125. Brookings Institution, Washington, DC.

Magnac, T. 1991. "Segmented or Competitive Labor Markets?" *Econometrica* 59: 165–87.

Manning, A. 2003. *Monopsony in Motion: Imperfect Competition in Labor Markets.* Princeton, NJ: Princeton University Press.

Micco, A., and C. Pages. 2006. "Employment Protection and Gross Job Flows: A Difference-In-Difference Approach." Mimeo. http://www-ilo-mirror.cornell. edu/public/english/bureau/integration/download/publicat/4_3_344_wb- _iadb_paper_on_employment_protection_and_gross_job_flows_pci_ meeting_june_2005.pdf

Murphy, K. M., and F. Welch. 1993. "Occupational Change and the Demand for Skill, 1940–1990." *American Economic Review, Papers and Proceedings* 83: 122–26.

Ngai, L. R., and C. A. Pissarides. 2004. "Structural Change in a Multi-Sector Model of Growth." Discussion Paper Series No. 4763. CEPR (Centre for Economic Policy Research), London, England.

Nickell, S. 1996. "Unemployment and Wages in Europe and North America." Discussion Paper Series No. 6. Centre for Economic Performance, University of Oxford.

Osmani, S. R. 2005. *The Employment Nexus between Growth and Poverty—An Asian Perspective.* Swedish International Development Cooperation Agency. Stockholm, Sweden.

Paci, R., and F. Pigliary. 1999. "Is Dualism Still a Source of Convergence in Europe?" *Applied Economics* 31 (11): 1423–36.

Peek, P. 2006, "Decent Work Deficits around the Globe: Measuring Trends with an Index." Geneva, Switzerland.

Poirson, H. 2000. "Factor Reallocation and Growth in Developing Countries." IMF Working Paper WP/00/94. IMF (International Monetary Fund), New York.

———. 2001. "The Impact of Intersectoral Labour Reallocation on Economic Growth." *Journal of African Economies* 10 (1): 37–63.

Psacharopoulos, G., and Z. Tzannatos. 1989. "Female Labor Force Participation: An International Perspective." *World Bank Research Observer* 4: 187–201.

Rama, M., and R. Artecona. 2002. "A Database of Labor Market Indicators Across Countries." Mimeo. http://www7.nationalacademies.org/internationallabor/ Rama_Artecona.pdf

Rao, D. S. P., T. J. Collelli, M. Alauddin. 2004. "Agricultural Productivity Growth and Poverty in Developing Countries, 1970–2000." ILO Employment Strategy Paper 2004/9. ILO, New York.

Ravallion, M. 1999. "Appraising Workfare." *World Bank Research Observer* 14: 31–48.

———. 2004. *Pro-Poor Growth: A Primer*. Washington, DC: World Bank Development Research Group Poverty Team.

———. 2005. *Inequality Is Bad for the Poor*. Washington, DC: World Bank Development Research Team.

Ravallion, M., and G. Datt. 2001. "Why Has Economic Growth Been More Pro-Poor in Some States of India than Others?" International Monetary Fund Seminar Series No. 2001-59. IMF, New York.

Ravallion, M., and M. Huppi. 1990. *The Sectoral Structure of Poverty during an Adjustment Period: Evidence for Indonesia in the Mid-1980s*. Washington, DC: Agriculture and Rural Development Department, World Bank.

Robertson, P. E. 1999. "Economic Growth and the Return to Capital in Developing Economies." *Oxford Economic Papers* 51 (4): 577–94.

Rodrik, D. 1997. "What Drives Public Employment?" NBER Working Paper 6141. NBER, Cambridge, MA.

Roy, A. D. 1951. "Some Thoughts on the Distribution of Earnings." *Oxford Economic Papers* 3: 135–46.

Saint-Paul, G. de 1996. *Dual Labor Markets: A Macroeconomic Perspective*. Cambridge, MA: MIT Press.

Sala-i-Martin, X. X. 1997. "I Just Ran Four Million Regressions." NBER Working Paper 6252. NBER, Cambridge, MA.

Satchi, M., and J. Temple. 2006. "Growth and Labor Markets in Developing Countries." Discussion paper. Department of Economics, University of Bristol, Bristol, England.

Schumpeter, J. A., and R. Opie. 1961. *The Theory of Economic Development: An Inquiry into Profits, Capital, Credit, Interest, and the Business Cycle*. New York: Oxford University Press.

Shorrocks, A. F. 1999. "Decomposition Procedures for Distributional Analysis: A Unified Framework Based on the Shapley Value." Mimeo. University of Essex, Essex, England.

Stark, O. 1990. *The Migration of Labor*. Oxford, England; Cambridge, MA: B. Blackwell.

Strauss, J. V., and D. Thomas. 1998. "Health, Nutrition, and Economic Development." *Journal of Economic Literature* 36: 766–817.

Temple, J., and L. Woessmann. 2004. "Dualism and Cross-Country Regressions." CESifo working paper. CESifo (Center for Economic Studies and Ifo Institute for Economic Research), Munich, Germany.

Wachter, M. L. 1974. "Primary and Secondary Labor Markets: A Critique of the Dual Approach." *Brookings Papers and Economic Activity* 3: 637–80.

World Bank. 2005. *Pro-Poor Growth in the 1990s. Lessons and Insights from 14 Countries*. Washington, DC: Agence Francaise pour le Development, Bundesministerium fur Wirtschaftlieche Zusammenrbeit, U.K. Department for International Development, and The World Bank.

———. 2006a. *Labor Mobility in Fourteen Countries*. Washington, DC: World Bank.

———. 2006b. "Good Jobs, Bad Jobs, No Jobs – Bringing More and Better Employment onto the Globalized Sahred-Gorwth Agenda." www.world bank. org/employment.

World Bank, Human Development Network Social Protection (HDNSP), Poverty Reduction and Economic Managment, Poverty Reduction Unit (PREMPR). 2006. "A Guide for Assessing Labor Market Conditions in Developing Countries." Mimeo. Washington, DC.

World Bank PREMPR. 2006a. "Review of Analytical Advisory Activities on Labor in the World Bank." Mimeo. Washington, DC.

———. 2006b. "Review of the Labor Content of Poverty Assessments and Poverty Reduction Strategy Papers in The World Bank." Mimeo. Washington, DC.

———. 2007. "Labor Diagnostics for Sub-Saharan Africa. Assessing Indicators and Data Available." Mimeo. Washington, DC.

# CHAPTER 2

# Employment in Low-Income Countries: Beyond Labor Market Segmentation?

## Gary S. Fields

### Introduction

People can be lifted out of poverty in a variety of ways: by consuming socially provided goods and services, by receiving transfers from family members, by moving to countries in which their labor would be better rewarded, or by earning their way out of poverty in the countries in which they live. In regard to social services, even with multilateral and bilateral assistance, the governments of low-income countries are too poor to be able to make a significant dent in poverty by the social services route alone. As for transfers, when most others around you are poor, private transfers are likely to be modest indeed. With respect to migration, countries in which labor earnings are higher do not exactly welcome the tired, the poor, and the huddled masses yearning to breathe free[1]—not any more and certainly not in large numbers. That leaves the creation of more and better earning opportunities for the poor as the only other available route out of poverty.[2]

This chapter offers some observations on policies for improving labor market and employment conditions in low-income countries. Before proceeding, some definitions are in order. *Labor markets* are the places in which labor services are bought and sold. *Employment* comprises both wage employment (in which the worker is hired by an employer and paid a wage or salary) and self-employment (including those who work on their own, who employ unpaid family members, or who hire others for pay to work along with them). As an empirical matter, the poorer the country, the more important self-employment is likely to be relative to wage employment. The International Labour Office (ILO) considers an individual to be employed if he or she worked at least 1 hour for pay or 15 hours not for pay in a family business or on a family farm in the reference week. In contrast to employment, the ILO defines an *unemployed* person as one (i) who was not engaged in even 1 hour of paid work or 15 hours of unpaid work in a family business or on a family farm in the reference week and (ii) was actively looking for work.

This chapter takes a segmented labor market approach to analyzing employment and unemployment in low-income countries' labor markets. *Labor market segmentation* is the idea that (i) the labor market consists of various segments with qualitatively distinct types of employment and (ii) access to the good job segments is limited in the sense that not all who want to work in those segments are able to be employed there. When there are just two segments, we have *labor market dualism*, which is best understood as a special case of labor market segmentation. Rationing of jobs in the good jobs sector is essential to the idea of labor market segmentation.

The segmented labor market approach stands as an alternative to two other strands in the literature. One is the single-sector labor market model or its close cousin, the integrated labor market model. The other is a model of multiple sectors with full choice among them.

The single-sector labor market model holds that workers are homogeneous and that they all participate in the same labor market. The basic labor market model presented in labor economics textbooks (e.g., Ehrenberg and Smith 2006; Borjas 2007) starts with these assumptions, as do the Ricardian and the Heckscher-Ohlin models, which are at the core of international trade (e.g., Bhagwati and Srinivasan 1983; Krugman and Obstfeld 2003). Both in labor economics and in international economics, more sophisticated models depart from the single-sector assumption.

The model closest to the single-sector models maintains that there are two sectors, but that wages and other terms and conditions of employment are the same in the two sectors (e.g., Krugman and Obstfeld 2003, p. 45). This model is sometimes called the "integrated labor market model." What all of these models have in common is that all jobs are equally attractive, and thus there is no such thing as "good jobs" and "bad jobs"—there are simply "jobs."

A third strand in the literature is the Roy (1951) model. Roy maintained that there are two sectors—he called them hunting and fishing—that are open in principle to all who would like to engage in either activity. Individuals allocate themselves between hunting and fishing according to comparative advantage. The payoffs to being in hunting and fishing in turn depend on the number of individuals choosing each sector. In equilibrium, the returns to the marginal worker in the two sectors are equalized.

In this chapter it is asserted that the single-sector model, the integrated labor market model, and the Roy model are descriptively inaccurate and therefore incapable of being used for analyzing low-income countries' labor markets or developing policies to improve conditions in them.

This chapter proceeds with a review of the intellectual history of dualism and segmentation. It then proceeds to discuss the importance of policy-relevant labor market models and offers suggestions on how they might be improved. A brief conclusion follows.

## Dualism and Segmentation in the History of Economic Thought

This chapter is influenced heavily by two well-developed strands of work in economics: the dual economy models of development economics and the dual labor market models of labor economics. At the same time, it is argued here that we need a third duality: the duality that arises *within* what is often called the informal sector (to be defined below). Bringing together these three types of duality into a coherent analytical framework is a task that lies at the frontier of research on labor markets and employment in low-income countries.

A half-century ago, two Nobel Prize-winning economists published two of the most influential papers in the history of development economics. The first was W. Arthur Lewis's path-breaking paper "Economic Development with Unlimited Supplies of Labour" (Lewis 1954).[3] Lewis wrote (p. 150): "Earnings in the subsistence sector set a floor to wages in the capitalist sector, but in practice wages have to be higher than this, and there is usually a gap of 30 per cent or more between capitalist wages and subsistence earnings." Lewis explained that although part of the gap is "illusory" because of the higher cost of living in the capitalist sector, there remained a real wage gap due to (i) the "psychological cost of transferring from the easy going way of life of the subsistence sector to the more regimented and urbanized environment of the capitalist sector," (ii) the payoff to experience in the capitalist sector, and (iii) "workers in the capitalist sector acquiring tastes and a social prestige which have conventionally to be recognized by higher real wages." Lewis went on to analyze the dynamics of economic growth as profits earned in the high-income sector were reinvested, leading to capital formation, an increased demand for labor, and continued intersectoral shifts.

Also in 1954, Simon Kuznets delivered his famous presidential address to the American Economic Association titled "Economic Growth and Income Inequality," published a few months later in Kuznets (1955). Kuznets explored how various measures of income inequality would change as the high-income sector comes to employ an increasing share of the population. All of the inequality measures used by Kuznets exhibited an inverted-U pattern, which later came to be known as the "Kuznets Curve."

Some of the subsequent writings on labor market dualism were grounded in the then-emergent theory of human capital, which earned its developers the Nobel Prize as well (Schultz 1961; Becker 1964).[4] The later literature on labor market dualism stressed that for dualism to exist, different wages must be paid in different sectors to *comparable* workers (e.g., Wachter 1974; Cain 1976). Many researchers reported empirical evidence showing such dualism or segmentation for observationally equivalent workers (e.g., Fields 1980). The extent to which such differences merely reflect unmeasured human capital was unknown then and still remains open to debate (e.g., Rosenzweig 1988).

Also in the 1970s, dual labor market theory received a boost through the work of Doeringer and Piore (1970). As summarized by Wachter (1974, p. 639), the dual labor market model advances four hypotheses:

> First, it is useful to dichotomize the economy into a primary and a secondary sector. Second, the wage and employment mechanisms in the secondary sector are distinct from those in the primary sector. Third, economic mobility between these two sectors is sharply limited, and hence workers in the secondary sector are essentially trapped there. Finally, the secondary sector is marked by pervasive underemployment because workers who could be trained for skilled jobs at no more than the usual cost are confined to unskilled jobs.

These features continue to be useful today, a point that is returned to later.

For some purposes, it is useful to think of just two labor market segments. These have alternatively been called capitalist and subsistence, formal and informal, modern and traditional, industry and agriculture, urban and rural, secondary and primary, and good and bad jobs. It is important to recognize that as a practical matter, none of these dichotomies is exactly the same as any other one.

Although many researchers continued to work within the dualistic framework (e.g., Harris and Todaro 1970; Stiglitz 1976), other researchers felt that another sector was needed. What Lewis, Kuznets, Harris and Todaro, and others all omitted was the apparent duality *within* the urban economy: some urban jobs were highly desirable and others were not. This in turn led to models with three types of employment—an urban formal sector, an urban informal sector,[5] and a rural agricultural sector— plus unemployment (e.g., Fields 1975). In these models, the best jobs were assumed to be located in the urban formal sector. Job seekers would therefore have an incentive to locate in the urban areas to improve their chances of being hired for the better jobs. However, in low-income countries, in which family resources are limited and unemployment benefits nonexistent, few job seekers could afford to remain unemployed and earn nothing for very long. The urban informal sector was seen as playing the important role of offering earning opportunities to such people. Accordingly, the urban informal sector was not only characterized, but in fact defined, as a free-entry or fall-back sector, one that enabled those who worked there to eke out a meager existence, not because they were happy about what they could earn there but because working and earning in the informal sector was better for most of them than being openly unemployed. Once the existence of a low-earning, free-entry sector was recognized, the view of the employment challenge in developing countries changed from a concern with employing the unemployed to the additional concern of raising the earnings of those employed (Turnham 1971; ILO 1972; Squire 1981). The ILO now reckons that there are seven times as many working poor in the world as there are unemployed (ILO 2007).

Defining the informal sector as a place in which all who want to work can gain entry and achieve what is typically a very modest level of earnings is not without controversy. Alternative definitions abound. The ILO (1972) defined informal activities as being characterized by (i) ease of entry; (ii) reliance on indigenous resources; (iii) family ownership of enterprises; (iv) small scale of operation; (v) labor-intensive and adapted technology; (vi) skills acquired outside the formal school system; and (vii) unregulated and competitive markets.[6] Souza and Tokman (1976) adopted as a working definition the following groups: the self-employed with less than 13 years of education; unpaid family members, employees, and employers in establishments of less than 10 employees; and domestic servants. Another commonly used definition is that suggested by DeSoto (1986), who regarded the informal sector as operating beyond the prevailing legal and institutional frameworks. At present, all of these definitions and others are used (Tokman 2001; Guha-Khasnobis, Kanbur, and Ostrom 2006), a fact that makes communication among analysts difficult.

More recently, one more feature of segmented labor markets has become apparent. That is the recognition of a fundamental duality that is found *within* the informal sector. On the one hand, the informal sector has free-entry activities of the sort described above. On the other hand, it also has restricted entry activities that people who could be working formally *choose* to work in instead. Fields (1990) highlighted this distinction and labeled these two components the "free entry" part of the informal sector and the "upper tier" of the informal sector. Recently, in a series of papers, William Maloney has maintained that, in Mexico at least, self-employment in the informal sector provides a package of wages, nonwage benefits, and working conditions that is at least as attractive for many people as what they could receive as wage employees in the formal sector (e.g., Maloney 2003, 2004). Still, though, there is "no consensus" (Maloney's term) on how many enterprises and individuals are to be found in each tier.

For labor market segmentation to exist, it is not enough that there be different types of employment. It must also be that the number of jobs in the better sectors is insufficient to employ all who would like to work there. The available jobs must be rationed among the job seekers, either in a random way as in the Harris-Todaro model or in a systematic way using characteristics such as education, gender, race, or tribe to include some individuals while excluding others.

The good jobs/bad jobs dichotomy is now being used by, among others, the World Bank (World Bank 2006), the ILO (current), the Inter-American Development Bank (IADB 2004), and the Asian Development Bank (2005). The evidence that the number of good jobs is insufficient for all who want and could perform them seems to be overwhelming.

In sum, the academic and the policy literatures have reached very substantial (but not unanimous) agreement on the proposition that developing countries' labor markets are segmented in the sense that (i) there exist distinct types of jobs and (ii) access to the relatively attractive jobs is limited. In the next section the implications of this position for labor market modeling are considered.

## Improving Policy-Relevant Labor Market Models

I have long maintained that good labor market policies require good labor market models and that good labor market modeling involves three components: sound theoretical formulations, appropriate empirical evidence, and careful welfare economics. This section addresses each of those components.

The literature reviewed in the preceding section leads to the conclusion that low-income countries' labor markets consist of at least five labor market states. Workers might be employed (be it in wage employment or self-employment) in one of four sectors: the formal sector, the free entry part of the urban informal sector, the upper tier of the urban informal sector, and rural agriculture. They might also be unemployed.

It seems that there do not yet exist rigorous labor market models that incorporate all five of these labor market states. The development of such models merits high priority in future research.

In addition to positing a multiplicity of sectors, segmented labor market models maintain that access to jobs in the better sectors is limited in the sense that not enough jobs are available for all who would like to work in those sectors and who are capable of doing so. An analytical starting point for segmented labor market models would be to model the case in which workers are homogeneous but sectors are not. Then, at a later stage, researchers could introduce skill differentials among workers and formulate models of how workers who differ in skills are matched with the better and the poorer employment opportunities.

In formulating such segmented labor market models, two questions need to be asked. The first is, how are wages and employment determined within each segment? And second, what mechanisms connect the segments?

It has proved useful to divide the analysis into three parts: modeling formal sector labor markets, modeling informal sector labor markets, and modeling the interrelationships between the formal and the informal sectors. There are at least four options for modeling the labor market in the formal sector: the supply-demand model with market wage determination, above-market-clearing wages set by institutional forces, above-market-clearing wages set by efficiency wage considerations, and above-market-clearing wages set by worker-side considerations.

As for the informal sector, three major options are available: informal work as employment of last resort, informal work as a preferred option, and the informal sector having its own internal dualism. Finally, the various sectors may be linked to one another in any of a number of ways—among them, the integrated labor market model, the crowding model, and the Harris-Todaro model. These various theoretical models are detailed in a guide to multisector labor market models (Fields 2005), to which the interested reader is referred.

Better theoretical models of low-income countries' labor markets are needed, but they are not enough. Good labor market modeling also requires empirical work at the appropriate level to inform these theoretical models. For labor market segmentation to exist, not only must the labor market consist of multiple segments, but also access to the better segments must be rationed. Information is needed on the determinants of employment in the good jobs sectors. At issue is not *which* people obtain the available jobs—we already know that these jobs go disproportionately to the better-educated, to men, and to members of favored ethnic or tribal groups. At issue is whether the demand for workers in good jobs is less than the available supply (which it most certainly seems to be) and, if so, why (the problem may well be that there are too many factors involved, not too few).[7]

As such empirical evidence comes in, we can expect to find that no one model will fit all low-income countries or perhaps even a majority of them. Which model fits which country is at this point an open question. And it may well be that the grouping of countries into different categories of models will reflect none of the standard typologies, such as open versus closed economy, natural resource rich versus natural resource poor, or African versus South Asian.

Finally, besides sound theoretical foundations and appropriate empirical evidence, good labor market policy models require good welfare economics. In the labor market area, the objective should *not* be to minimize unemployment. It is now widely recognized that the concept of unemployment has serious (some would say fatal) flaws—among them, the fact that few very poor people can afford to be unemployed for any substantial amount of time and the fact that being employed does not ensure an adequate income or other aspects of a standard of living. For this reason, the director-general of the ILO has long called for closing the "decent work deficit" (e.g., ILO 1999), and the organization is now proposing an index of labor market well-being (in its terminology, a "decent work index") that includes not only the unemployment rate but also seven other indicators with equal weight (Peek 2006).[8] Similarly, the World Bank is piloting a study of 35 labor market indicators in eight countries, in which how much one earns when employed rather than the fact of employment per se features prominently (World Bank 2006). Labor market specialists know that the unemployment rate is a problematical measure in the context of low-income countries, but the message has not gone out sufficiently to nonspecialists in operations and elsewhere.

A less obvious implication of the existence of labor market segmentation in low-income countries has to do with the employment elasticity of output.[9] The employment elasticity of output is defined as the percentage increase in employment associated with a 1 percent increase in output.[10] However, the resultant output elasticity of employment is virtually meaningless as an indicator of the goodness or badness of labor market conditions. Why? Because in a low-income country, employment is determined much more by the growth of the working-age population than it is by the willingness of employers to hire people. Many indicators of labor market conditions are meaningful in a low-income country context, but the output elasticity of employment is not one of them.

In sum, good policy-relevant labor market modeling requires sound theoretical models, empirical evidence, and welfare economics.

## Concluding Remarks

This chapter has conveyed the author's sympathy for segmented labor market models. It seems evident that for workers of any given skill type, there are better jobs and worse jobs, and the number of good jobs is limited. In trying to achieve the highest utility attainable, most workers in low-income countries may be presumed to desire the highest-paying jobs, although some may prefer jobs that offer greater autonomy, flexibility, or other nonincome benefits. None of the other alternatives—that there is a single sector; that there are multiple sectors but the returns to labor are the same in each of them; and that an unlimited number of jobs of each type are available to all who want them, and each worker chooses the job in which he or she has a comparative advantage—appears to be realistic.

The segmented labor market model leads to policy conclusions that are different from other models. Labor market outcomes need to be judged not only on the basis of whether workers are employed but also on the basis of the quality of the jobs in which they are employed.

Take the international trade field as an example. If all jobs were the same for workers in a given skill category, then a worker who loses his or her job in one sector could take up a comparable job in another sector with essentially no loss in pay. But not all jobs are the same, and typically the workers who lose from international competition suffer significant earnings losses, often very substantial ones (Uchitelle 2006). As a result, it is no longer acceptable to base trade policy on national aggregates alone—even if the country as a whole is better off, not all individuals within it are. It is for this reason that publications across the political spectrum (including *The Wall Street Journal, The Economist,* and *The New York Times*) and economists of all political persuasions (including Bhagwati, Panagariya, and Srinivasan 2004; Blanchard 2005; Kletzer 2005; Stiglitz 2006) are now calling for policies such as expanded trade adjustment assistance and wage insurance to compensate those who lose as a result of globalization. The field of labor economics would benefit from an even closer partnership between labor market modelers and trade policy modelers.

In policy discussions, two mistakes are frequently made. Some analysts maintain that policy interventions need to be made in the sectors of the economy in which the poor *are,* so as to raise their earnings there. Other analysts maintain that the most appropriate interventions are in the parts of the economy in which the poor *are not,* so that more of the poor can be drawn into the higher-earning parts of the economy.[11] Neither of these conclusions—that development efforts should be concentrated on the sectors in which the poor *are* or on the sectors in which the poor *are not*—is implied by the data, nor is either conclusion necessarily correct. Sometimes, the best policy course will be to provide people with complementary inputs so that they can earn more in the sectors they are in, whereas other times the best course will be to enlarge other sectors of the economy so that the poor can move in. What is required in choosing between these alternatives is a careful comparison of the social benefits and costs associated with each policy option in a given country context. More social cost-benefit analysis should be performed in the labor market area than is usually done.

This chapter substantiates seven assertions. First, segmentation of labor markets is virtually ubiquitous in low-income countries; we cannot do without it in formulating policies. Second, such segmentation is of a higher order than mere dualism. Third, the dimensions of labor markets that are important to understand are the forces determining wages and employment in each sector as well as the connections between sectors. Fourth, the theoretical foundations for segmented labor market analysis are supply and demand, market-clearing and non-market-clearing equilibriums, institutional forces, and intermarket connections. Fifth, what the empirical evidence tells us is that a single-market framework will not do. Sixth, informality is essential to understanding employment in low-income countries. And seventh, informality, if precisely defined and suitably qualified, is a useful concept. However, because the term "informal sector" means different things to different people, it may be better to abandon the term and use alternatives such as "free-entry sector," "unregistered sector," or "microenterprises" instead.

To conclude, as the evidence is interpreted here, the good jobs in a typical low-income country are primarily the formal sector jobs, and not everybody who would like a formal sector job can get one. Accordingly, the dual challenge for policy is to find ways of creating more good jobs while also raising the labor market earnings of those who are rationed out of the good jobs sector and have the opportunity to work only in the bad jobs sector. For the low-income countries of the world, these are very large challenges indeed.

## Notes

1. The phrasing is from Emma Lazarus's poem ("The New Colossus") on the pedestal of the Statue of Liberty in the United States.

2. *Earning Their Way Out of Poverty* is the title of my next book.

3. See also the elaboration of the Lewis model by Fei and Ranis (1964).

4. See also Mincer (1974).

5. Often called "urban traditional sector."

6. This definition is ambiguous because it is not clear whether all of these characteristics must hold for the enterprise to be regarded as informal or whether any one of them would suffice.

7. The World Bank's MILES framework raises a whole range of important issues, empirical knowledge of which would contribute to understanding the level of demand for workers in good jobs. This framework includes the following components with respective policy issues: macroeconomic conditions (conditions for growth and macroeconomic stability); investment climate (regulatory environment, government transparency, taxes, financing, infrastructure, and legal environment); labor market policies and institutions (labor market regulation, wage setting, and nonwage costs); education and skills (basic education, higher education and training, and lifelong learning); and a safety net for workers.

8. The seven other components in addition to the unemployment rate are the employment-to-population ratio, average earnings per worker, percentage of working poor, government social security expenditures as a percentage of

GDP, percentage of children economically active, gender gap in labor force participation, and gap in ratifications of ILO standards.

9. See for example Kapsos (2005), who lists employment elasticities for 160 economies. Sundaram and Tendulkar (2002) discuss other shortcomings of this approach.

10. Ordinarily, output in the economy is measured as real GDP and employment is measured as the number of people employed in the economy. To repeat, the ILO classifies a person as employed if he or she worked 1 hour or more for pay or 15 hours or more not for pay in the reference week.

11. Achieving economic development by moving people out of the poorer sectors and into the richer ones has been labeled "intersectoral shifts." Both the Lewis and the Kuznets models described above are models of intersectoral shifts. These and later contributions are reviewed in Basu (1997).

## References

ADB (Asian Development Bank). 2005. *Labor Markets in Asia: Promoting Full, Productive, and Decent Employment.* Manila: ADB.

Basu, Kaushik. 1997. *Analytical Development Economics.* Cambridge, MA: MIT Press.

Becker, Gary S. 1964. *Human Capital.* New York: Columbia University Press for the National Bureau of Economic Research.

Bhagwati, Jagdish N., Arvind Panagariya, and T. N. Srinivasan. 2004. "The Muddles Over Outsourcing." *Journal of Economic Perspectives* 18 (4): 93–114.

Bhagwati, Jagdish N., and T. N. Srinivasan. 1983. *Lectures on International Trade.* Cambridge, MA: MIT Press.

Blanchard, Olivier. 2005. "European Unemployment: The Evolution of Facts and Ideas." NBER Working Paper No. 11750. NBER (National Bureau of Economic Research), Cambridge, MA.

Borjas, George. 2007. *Labor Economics.* New York: McGraw Hill.

Cain, Glen. 1976. "The Challenge of Segmented Labor Market Theories to Orthodox Theory: A Survey." *Journal of Economic Literature* (December): 1215–57.

DeSoto, Hernando. 1986. *El Otro Sendero: La Revolución Informal.* Lima, Peru: Instituto Libertad y Democracia.

Doeringer, Peter B., and Michael J. Piore. 1970. *Internal Labor Markets and Manpower Analysis.* Lexington, KY: Heath.

Ehrenberg, Ronald G., and Robert S. Smith. 2006. *Modern Labor Economics,* 9th ed. Boston, MA: Pearson Addison Wesley.

Fei, John C. H., and Gustav Ranis. 1964. *Development of the Labor Surplus Economy*. Homewood, IL: Irwin.

Fields, Gary S. 1975. "Rural-Urban Migration, Urban Unemployment and Underemployment, and Job Search Activity in LDCs." *Journal of Development Economics* 2: 165–88.

———. 1980. "Education and Income Distribution in Developing Countries: A Review of the Literature." In *Education and Income*, ed. Timothy King. Washington, DC: World Bank.

———. 1990. "Labor Market Modeling and the Urban Informal Sector: Theory and Evidence." In *The Informal Sector Revisited*, ed. David Turnham, Bernard Salomé, and Antoine Schwarz. Paris: OECD (Organisation for Economic Co-operation and Development).

———. 2005. "A Guide to Multisector Labor Market Models." World Bank Social Protection Unit Discussion Paper No. 0505. World Bank, Washington, DC.

Guha-Khasnobis, Basudeb, Ravi Kanbur, and Elinor Ostrom. 2006. *Linking the Formal and the Informal Economy*. Oxford, England: Oxford University Press.

Harris, John, and Michael Todaro. 1970. "Migration, Unemployment, and Development: A Two Sector Analysis." *American Economic Review* 40: 126–42.

IADB (Inter-American Development Bank). 2004. *Good Jobs Wanted*. Washington, DC: IADB.

ILO (International Labour Office). 1972. *Employment, Incomes and Equality*. Geneva, Switzerland: ILO.

———. 1999. *Report of the Director-General: Decent Work*. Report presented at the 87th session of the International Labour Conference, Geneva, Switzerland, June.

———. 2007. *Global Employment Trends*. Geneva, Switzerland: ILO.

———. Current. http://www.ilo.org/public/english/decent.htm.

Kapsos S. 2005. "The Employment Intensity of Growth: Trends and Macroeconomic Determinants." ILO Employment Strategy Papers 2005/12. ILO, Geneva, Switzerland.

Kletzer, Lori. 2005. "Trade-Related Job Loss and Wage Insurance: A Synthetic Review." *Review of International Economics* 12 (5).

Krugman, Paul R., and Maurice Obstfeld. 2003. *International Economics*, 6th ed. Boston, MA: Addison Wesley.

Kuznets, Simon. 1955. "Economic Growth and Income Inequality." *American Economic Review* 45: 1–28.

Lewis, W. Arthur. 1954. "Economic Development with Unlimited Supplies of Labour." *Manchester School* 22: 139–91.

Maloney, William. 2003. "Informal Self-Employment: Poverty Trap or Decent Alternative?" In *Pathways Out of Poverty*, ed. Gary S. Fields and Guy Pfeffermann. Boston, MA: Kluwer.

———. 2004. "Informality Revisited." *World Development* 32 (7): 1159–78.

Mincer, Jacob. 1974. *Schooling, Experience, and Earnings*. New York: NBER.

Peek, Peter. 2006. "Decent Work Deficits Around the Globe: Measuring Trends with an Index." Mimeo, Geneva, Switzerland: ILO.

Rosenzweig, Mark. 1988. "Labor Markets in Low Income Countries: Distortions, Mobility, and Migration" In *Handbook of Development Economics*, ed. Hollis Chenery and T. N. Srinivasan. Elsevier. Amsterdam.

Roy, A. D. 1951. "Some Thoughts on the Distribution of Earnings." *Oxford Economic Papers* 3: 135–46.

Schultz, T. W. 1961. "Investment in Human Capital." *American Economic Review.* LI: 1–17.

Souza, Paulo R., and Victor E. Tokman. 1976. "The Informal Urban Sector in Latin America." *International Labour Review* 114 (3): 355–65.

Squire, Lyn. 1981. *Employment Policy in Developing Countries*. New York: Oxford University Press for the World Bank.

Stiglitz, Joseph E. 1976. "The Efficiency Wage Hypothesis, Surplus Labor, and the Distribution of Labour in LDCs." *Oxford Economic Papers* 28: 185–207.

———. 2006. *Making Globalization* Work. New York: Norton.

Sundaram K., and Suresh K. Tendulkar. 2002 "The Working Poor in India: Employment-Poverty Linkages and Employment Poverty Options." Issues in Employment and Poverty Discussion Paper 4, ILO, Geneva, Switzerland.

Tokman, Victor. 2001. "Integrating the Informal Sector into the Modernization Process." *SAIS Review* 21 (1): 45–60.

Turnham, David. 1971. *The Employment Problem in Less Developed Countries*. Paris: Development Centre of the Organisation for Economic Co-Operation and Development.

Uchitelle, Louis. 2006. *The Disposable American: Layoffs and Their Consequences*. New York: Knopf.

Wachter, Michael. 1974. "Primary and Secondary Labor Markets: A Critique of the Dual Approach." *Brookings Papers on Economic Activity* 3: 637–80.

World Bank. 2006. "Good Jobs, Bad Jobs, No Jobs—Bringing More and Better Employment onto the Globalized Shared-Growth Agenda." www.world bank.org/employment.

# CHAPTER 3

# Good Jobs, Bad Jobs, and Economic Performance: A View from the Middle East and North Africa Region

## Samir Radwan

## Introduction

The controversy about good jobs and bad jobs has gained importance with the recent wave of globalization. At the center of the debate is the concern that increased international competition may lower the earnings and negatively affect the working conditions of the most vulnerable workers while benefiting the rest.

Good jobs are tantamount to "decent" work, defined by the International Labour Organization (ILO) as "productive work with the protection of rights, adequate pay, social coverage and the presence of social dialogue, freedom of association, collective bargaining, and participation" (ILO 2001). Though this chapter asserts that bad jobs are not perfectly synonymous with informality, a significant overlap between the two exists in the Middle East and North Africa region.[1]

As highlighted in the preceding chapter by Gary Fields, there is no academic consensus on characterizations of the informal sector and informal employment. It can alternatively be considered as a survival strategy for the poor or as a breeding ground of entrepreneurship that could flourish if only it were not burdened with unnecessary regulations and bureaucracy. Or it can be viewed as a vast sector that escapes regulation and a repository of bad jobs that lack the minimum attributes of what is defined as decent work.

This chapter joins the debate from the perspective of the Middle East and North Africa region. It substantiates three principal assertions: first, that the rate and pattern of growth in the region have not solved the problem of lack of employment; second, that most of the jobs created are found in the informal economy, which is associated mainly (but not exclusively) with bad jobs; and third, that the major challenge for the region is to create 5 million good jobs a year during the next 20 years.

Briefly surveying relevant theoretical perspectives on the informal sector, the chapter than examines the extent and nature of informal employment in the Middle East and North Africa region. The chapter concludes by suggesting some policy routes that might resolve the essential dilemma posed by the growth of the informal sector in the region (ILO 1991).

## Informal Sector: An Antipoverty Strategy or an Engine of Growth?

The traditional view of the informal sector characterizes it as marginal in regard to size and contribution to the economy; it is also seen as a transitory stage for those waiting to be formally employed. However, this view has been revised significantly. More than three decades of careful observance have revealed that the informal sector has maintained its lead in employment and increased its relative share in many economies. However, controversy over the contribution of this sector to the welfare of the economy remains.

Three principal standpoints are encapsulated by the debate. The first view, also characterized by Fields in chapter 2 as an extension of the dualist approach, portrays the urban informal sector as a free entry repository of bad jobs, lacking the decent conditions usually associated with the regulated sector. Labor market segmentation, according to this point of view, precludes mobility between the formal and informal economy. The second point of view, by contrast, characterizes the informal sector as a breeding ground for flourishing microentrepreneurship and not a mere residual of the formal sector. Maloney (2004) argues that evidence from Mexico suggests that the share of the workforce in self-employment grew even as the self-employed went from earning roughly the same amount as formal salaried workers to 30 percent more by 1992.

According to this second viewpoint, low earnings are not an exclusive characteristic of the informal sector, nor are bad jobs perfectly synonymous with the informal economy. Some informal enterprises are highly productive, efficient, and organized and informal employment is often voluntary. In some cases, informal enterprises are more capable of growing and increasing their productivity than formal ones, and the smaller size of informal enterprises is sometimes more conducive to the nourishment of learning by the constituents and enhances their ability to absorb and improve on the required skills. It follows that the informal sector is not always the result of labor market segmentation: "It may be the attractiveness of informal self-employment that causes dualism, rather than segmented markets causing informality . . . The point here is not to show that the informal sector never serves as safety net, but rather, that for the most part, entrepreneurs want to be in the sector, and that it should not be treated as inherently inferior" (Maloney 2004).

A third position on the informal economy is provided by De Soto (1989), who argues that it has high potential but is stifled by government regulations and even harassment. In his analysis, the emergence of the informal sector is seen partly as a response to high transaction costs, formal regulations, and bureaucracy, which limited the access of firms to resources and capital and made functioning on an informal basis more attractive for entrepreneurs. De Soto also argues that there is little awareness of the large amount of capital possessed by those working in the informal sector. He states that "ownership cannot be readily traced and validated, and exchanges cannot be governed by a legally recognized set of rules, their assets cannot be used in efficient and legally secured market transactions. Their property is in effect, 'dead capital'" (De Soto 1989). He estimates, for instance, that informal entrepreneurs in Egypt own about US$240 billion of dead capital (or two and half times the GDP). The ability of the informal sector to contribute positively to economic growth is severely curtailed.

These various characterizations of the informal sector are not merely issues of academic debate. Rather, what constitutes appropriate policy will vary widely according to how this sector is viewed. For instance, the first view would imply that making more decent jobs available depends on both formal sector employment creation and policies (such as education, training and labor regulation reforms) to address barriers to mobility between the two sectors. The second view might suggest a policy approach that looks at labor-intensive informal enterprises with low capital requirements to contribute to the objective of poverty reduction through employment generation. For his part, De Soto (1997) advocates formalization as the ultimate solution for invigorating the economic potential of informal enterprises.

The rest of this chapter contributes to the debate by offering a regional insight into whether bad jobs are perfectly synonymous with informality. It asserts that the two are not perfectly congruent but largely overlapping in the Middle East and North Africa region and considers appropriate policy responses to the developmental issues posed by bad, informal jobs.

## A Comparative Profile of the Informal Sector

This section offers a brief overview of the size, significance, and composition of the informal sector in the Middle East and North Africa, relative to other developing regions. According to the ILO, informal employment comprises one-half to three-quarters of nonagricultural employment in the developing countries: 48 percent in North Africa, 51 percent in Latin America, 65 percent in Asia, and 72 percent in Sub-Saharan Africa.[2] The figure for the North African region is an average of four countries: Algeria, Morocco, Tunisia, and Egypt. It is highest in Egypt, in which informal employment stands at 55 percent of nonagricultural employment, followed by 50 percent in Tunisia and 45 percent in Morocco; the least share was found in Algeria, standing at 43 percent (see table 3.1).

The estimated average (unweighted) share of the informal sector in nonagricultural GDP is 27 percent in North Africa. This percentage is low compared with other developing regions—it is as high as 41 percent in Sub-Saharan Africa. (However, such statistics should be taken with caution when used in cross-country comparisons because of the disparities in the accounting systems.) During the 1990s nonagricultural informal employment grew steadily. This is typical of developing countries that have undergone economic reforms and, in particular, public sector retrenchment policies (discussed in greater detail below).

Looking at the distribution of the informal employment by sex, we find that women's informal employment in the North Africa region as a percentage of women's nonagricultural employment is the lowest among the other developing regions. It stands at 43 percent, whereas it reaches as high

**Table 3.1. Informal Employment as Percentage of Nonagricultural Employment in Selected Developing Regions**

| | Informal employment as percentage of nonagricultural employment | Women's informal employment as percentage of women's nonagricultural employment | Men's informal employment as percentage of men's nonagricultural employment |
|---|---|---|---|
| North Africa | 48 | 43 | 49 |
| Algeria | 43 | 41 | 43 |
| Morocco | 45 | 47 | 44 |
| Tunisia | 50 | 39 | 53 |
| Egypt | 55 | 46 | 57 |
| Sub-Saharan Africa | 72 | 84 | 63 |
| Latin America | 51 | 58 | 48 |
| Asia | 65 | 65 | 65 |

*Source:* ILO 2002b.

as 84 percent in Sub-Saharan Africa. In Latin America and Asia this percentage is 58 percent and 65 percent, respectively. In North Africa, men's informal employment as a percentage of their nonagricultural employment is 49 percent.[3] North Africa is thus the only one of the four developing regions in which this percentage is lower among women than among men.

In accordance with other developing regions, in North Africa self-employment constitutes a larger share of total nonagricultural informal employment (62 percent) than does wage employment (38 percent). Thus North Africa ranks second after Sub-Saharan Africa, in which self-employment accounts for 70 percent of informal employment.[4] Distributed by sex, self-employment seems to be more important among women than among men across all regions except for Latin America. In North Africa, 72 percent of informally employed women outside the agricultural sector are self-employed; this figure is 60 percent among men.

Nonagricultural self-employment in North Africa is higher in trade (40 percent) than in industry (33 percent) and services (28 percent), similar to how it is in Sub-Saharan Africa and Asia (ILO 2002b). For women, the highest self-employment rate is found in industry (52 percent of total nonagricultural self-employed women), whereas 26 percent and 22 percent are employed in the trade and the services sectors, respectively. This can be attributed to social norms that constrain women's ability to participate in activities outside their homes and result in a relatively high incidence of women working at home in manufacturing activities (ILO 2002b).

## Why Do Bad Jobs and Informal Jobs Overlap?

The academic debates about the nature of informality referred to at the beginning of this chapter indicate that informal sector jobs are not necessarily bad jobs. However, in the case of the Middle East and North Africa region, the two overlap. This section first provides an explanation for a broad coincidence of bad and informal jobs in the Middle East and North Africa, and then it offers an intraregional nuance to these arguments.

The division of good and bad jobs between the formal and informal sectors, respectively, is not entirely clear-cut in the region. For example, the "working poor" (who earn less than the poverty income of US$1 per day per capita) can be found in both formal and informal jobs (ILO 2001). Moreover, in some countries in the Middle East and North Africa, social security coverage is limited to only a small proportion of workers in the formal sector. Nonetheless, informal jobs represent the predominant repository of bad jobs in the region.

One of the major reasons for the proliferation of informal employment in the Middle East and North Africa has been the decline of public sector employment. During the 1990s, average government employment in the Middle East and North Africa was the highest in the world (more than 17 percent), slightly exceeding the Organisation for Economic Co-operation and Development (OECD) average and going way beyond that of Asia and Latin America (about 6 percent and 9 percent, respectively). As large public wage bills eventually came to be deemed an unsustainable burden on public finances, there were several attempts at downsizing public employment. In some cases, the downsizing of the public sector was almost exactly correlated with a rise in informality. For instance, a gradual informalization in Egypt is evidenced in the decrease in the proportion of new entrants going directly into public sector employment. In the 1970s this proportion hovered between 60 and 70 percent, but by 1998, it had fallen to 25 percent. Meanwhile the share of new entrants whose first jobs were informal increased from less than 20 percent in the 1970s to 60 percent in the late 1990s, nearly matching the decline in the public sector share (World Bank 2003).

It is evident from these statistics that the pace of formal private sector employment creation has not been sufficient to create opportunities for all entrants into the labor market. Informal businesses suffer from several challenges, including difficulties in dealing with local authorities and access to infrastructure, credit, and technology. Formal enterprises face a different set of obstacles, including the complex bureaucratic procedures needed to start a business, operate it, and close it down, if necessary. These difficulties, along with others like taxes, are among the major reasons behind the slow growth of formal sector employment.

Incentives are often skewed against formalization, the prevalence of informal housing being a case in point. In a study conducted by De Soto on the informal sector in Egypt, it was found that 92 percent of urban housing units and 87 percent of those in rural areas were informal property. Informal housing does not allow owners to use their property as collateral for credit, and their ownership is not guaranteed. Because it cannot be sold, informal property represents unused resources—"dead capital" (De Soto quoted by Galal 2004). People have resorted to informally owning these units because of the complexity of bureaucratic procedures surrounding legal property ownership. In Egypt, for example, the registration of a publicly owned piece of land in the desert requires about 77 procedures that could take from 6 to 14 years. In addition, if an owner of an informal property decides to formalize his or her ownership, the owner risks being ordered to remove the unit or may even be sentenced to jail (Galal 2004).

Although, in theory, the informal sector could contribute to increased competitiveness in manufacturing, this has not been observed to be the case in the Middle East and North Africa. In some regions, products manufactured in highly organized informal enterprises have been fit for competition with those produced in the formal sector. Spurred on by the need to keep prices low so as to compete internationally, the formal sector has engaged in the outsourcing of production to smaller informal enterprises that are able to provide the required quality at cheaper prices.[5]

In the case of the Middle East and North Africa region, the competitiveness of the informal sector has been constrained by inherent weaknesses observed across almost all countries of the region (Abdel-Fadil 2002). First, informal enterprises tend to have an extremely low capital intensity, estimated to be less than one-tenth of that for medium- and large-scale enterprises (Handoussa and Potter 1992). This has resulted in lower labor productivity and, in turn, lower earnings per employee. Second, most of the small enterprises are operated as family businesses with little or no access to formal credit channels, thus limiting their capacity to grow. Third, working conditions in the informal sector tend not to meet international labor standards because of a lack of social protection, workweeks of 50 hours or more, the absence of minimal sanitary and safety regulations, and the frequent use of child labor.

A final reason for the concentration of bad jobs in the informal sector in the Middle East and North Africa is a mismatch in the skill level of supply and demand in the labor market. Historically, an overinflated public sector absorbed, at least partially, the share of the labor force that could not find employment in the formal private sector. Increasingly, the informal sector is fulfilling that role.

Table 3.2 illustrates part of the result of a survey conducted in 2001 in Egypt on the expected demand for labor during the 2001–2005 period, compared with the structure of supply. The survey revealed some serious imbalances, one of the most important of which was that the skills of the majority of the unemployed were not those skills needed and demanded by firms.

The table shows that demand for the unemployment category with intermediate education was minimal (4 percent) although they represented 55 percent of the unemployed. The bulk of demand (66 percent) was for those with below intermediate education, with only 17 percent of the demand for graduates of higher education (Radwan 2002).

**Table 3.2. Labor Force, Unemployment, and Labor Demand by Education Status in Egypt**

| Sector | Labor force* | | Unemployment** | | Labor demand*** | |
|---|---|---|---|---|---|---|
| | Thousand | % | Thousand | % | Thousand | % |
| Illiterate | 7,192 | 33 | 135 | 8 | | |
| Read and write | 2,076 | 9 | 73 | 4 | | |
| Below intermediate | 3,522 | 16 | 143 | 8 | 531 | 66 |
| Intermediate | 5,305 | 24 | 947 | 55 | 28 | 4 |
| Above intermediate | 1,267 | 6 | 181 | 11 | 108 | 13 |
| University and higher | 2,705 | 12 | 242 | 14 | 138 | 17 |
| Total | 22,061 | 100 | 1,721 | 100 | 805 | 100 |

*Source:* Labor Force and Unemployment: CAPMAS, Labor Market Demand: Labor Demand Survey in Labor Market, as cited in Radwan 2002.

* 1998 data; Represents persons at working age (6 year or more).

** 1998 data; Represents persons ages 15 or more.

*** Data for 2001–2005.

The reasons offered above for the intersection of bad and informal jobs in the Middle East and North Africa—public sector reforms, a regulatory environment that cramps private sector development, low competitiveness, and skills mismatches—are broadly applicable across the region. In addition, certain intraregional differences contribute to differences in the characteristics of the informal sector across countries. A useful distinction can be drawn between three types of economies: oil economies or Gulf Cooperation Council countries (GCC), labor surplus diversified economies (e.g., Egypt, Jordan, Morocco, Tunisia), and the marginalized poor economies (e.g., Sudan, Yemen, Somalia). Although bad informal sector jobs present a serious problem in all three groups, the causes of informality and the composition of the informal labor force vary somewhat according to country conditions.

In the GCC countries, only a small proportion of the expatriate workers have the same privileges that nationals have. They are subject to different restrictions, such as work permits, sponsorship permits, quotas, and employment fees, imposed on the recruitment of nonnational workers (Girgis 2002). Such measures limit the access of expatriate workers to good jobs in favor of nationals, effectively creating a subclass of foreign workers, concentrated in the informal sector. Table 3.3 shows the percentage of nationals and expatriates in the labor force of GCC countries.

In the labor surplus diversified economies, there is a proliferation of informal employment, the result primarily of inadequate growth, which

**Table 3.3. Share of Nationals and Expatriates in the Labor Force of GCC Countries**

|  | 1995 * | | | 2001** | | |
|---|---|---|---|---|---|---|
|  | Total (000s) | % Nationals | % Nonnationals | Total (000s) | % Nationals | % Nonnationals |
| UAE | 955.1 | 11.6 | 88.4 | 2,079.0 | 10.2 | 89.8 |
| Bahrain | 226.5 | 40.0 | 60.0 | 308.3 | 40.1 | 59.9 |
| KSA | 6,450.0 | 36.5 | 63.5 | 7,100.0*** | 50.0 | 50.0 |
| Oman | 670.3 | 35.8 | 64.2 | 704.9 | 20.7 | 79.2 |
| Qatar | 218.0 | 17.9 | 82.1 | 322.9 | 14.2 | 85.7 |
| Kuwait | 1,051.5 | 16.6 | 83.4 | 1,214.3 | 19.6 | 80.3 |
| **Total** | **9,571.4** | **26.4** | **73.6** | **11,729.4** | **26** | **74** |

*Sources:* * Maurice Girgis, *National Versus Migrant Workers in the GCC: Coping with Change*, 2002.
** GCC, *Statistical Bulletin*, Volume 12, 2003. http://www.gcc-sg.org/gccstatvo112/genstat/g4.htm.
*** *ILO Yearbook of Labor Statistics*, 2002.
UAE·= United Arab Emirates.
KSA = Kingdom of Saudi Arabia.

**Table 3.4. Labor Force and Unemployment in the Diversified Economies**

| Country | Average labor force growth (%) (1996–2001) | Labor force in millions (1995–2001) | Unemployment (%) 1995–2001 |
|---|---|---|---|
| Algeria | 3.4 | 9.60 | 28.7 |
| Egypt | 3.0 | 23.06 | 7.4 |
| Jordan | 4.1 | 1.35 | 13.7 |
| Lebanon | 2.7 | 1.45 | 8.4 |
| Morocco | 2.5 | 10.95 | 17.8 |
| Syria | 4.1 | 4.78 | 6.5 |
| Tunisia | 2.5 | 3.61 | 15.6 |

*Sources:* The Arab Monetary Fund, *Arab Unified Economic Report* (various issues). World Bank, *World Development Indicators* (various issues).

failed to create enough employment in the formal economy. Although the labor force grew by almost 3 percent on average during the period from 1995 to 2001, unemployment has risen by an average of 14 percent—but there is some variation across countries, as shown in table 3.4. In this case, the major problem is on the demand side of the labor market. Moreover, the employment problem is tied to many structural and microeconomic problems, most importantly the acquisition of skills, productivity, and human resource development, as well as the mismatch between labor supply and demand.

In the marginalized economies, the problem is that of both insufficient growth and inadequate social security coverage. Under such circumstances, informal, low-productivity employment becomes the refuge for the majority of workers who are usually locked up in a low-level poverty trap.

## Conclusion: The Dilemma of the Informal Sector

Understanding the drivers of growth of the informal sector is instrumental for rethinking the policies for dealing with it. In view of the arguments posed at the beginning of this chapter on the nature of the contribution of the informal sector to the economy, we can argue that, on the whole, the informal sector in the Middle East and North Africa region has been associated largely with bad jobs. In addition, open unemployment in the Middle East and North Africa has reached

15 percent on average, one of the highest rates in the world. The region is facing the enormous challenge of creating 100 million jobs by 2020, a doubling of the current level of employment in the first two decades of the 21st century (World Bank 2003a).

Informal employment in the Middle East and North Africa is at once a safety net and a reflection of the lack of the economic mobility of low-income groups. The Middle East and North Africa economies have not been able to generate enough growth to absorb new entrants into the labor market, resulting in the emergence of a large informal sector which has absorbed a sizable portion of the unemployed, in the absence of adequate social protection. Thus bad jobs in the informal sector have been created to cater primarily to low-income groups that are excluded from formal or decent employment. As Bourguignon (2005) has remarked, although some unemployed can afford to queue for a decent job, others will accept any kind of occupation that allows them to survive, even if it means working under harsh conditions.

The overlap between bad and informal jobs in the Middle East and North Africa leads us to reflect on the well-known dilemma of the informal sector. If the bad jobs in the Middle East and North Africa region are created mostly in the informal sector and they are not seen to be conducive to the desired development but eliminating them would contribute only to the aggravation of the unemployment problem, what is the way out? The ILO, in its report "The Dilemma of the Informal Sector," sums up the problem as follows: "Should the informal sector be allowed to continue to expand outside the frame work of laws and institutions governing social and economic life, and thus provide a convenient low-cost way of absorbing labor that cannot be employed elsewhere; or should attempts be made to bring it into the rest of society, with the risk of impairing its capacity to absorb labor?" (ILO 1991). This conclusion outlines possible policy responses to the dilemma of the informal sector with respect to the Middle East and North Africa region.

The comprehensive application of appropriate social security coverage and labor rights to all workers, irrespective of their status of formality, represents one possible policy response to the dilemma of the informal sector, in effect guaranteeing decent work conditions in both the formal and the informal sectors. Bourguignon (2005) suggests that decoupling labor market status and social protection as much as possible is part of the answer because it would reduce the distance between good and bad jobs. Implementation, however, does not promise to be simple, and this option seems to respond more to the situation in developed countries (Galal 2004).

A second policy choice is to extend labor market regulations to informal enterprises so as to bring them into the formal economy. An argument that was developed in the study of the economics of formalization in Egypt suggests that unless serious reforms are made on the administrative, legal, and economic front in order to increase the advantages of formalization relative to its disadvantages, informal businesses will never be attracted to formalization (Galal 2004). In Egypt's case, a set of comprehensive reforms that could be adopted to encourage formalization should include the simplification of all rules and procedures concerning entry, operation, expansion, and exit of firms. It would also include the creation of an independent organization to carry out the formalization process.

But is formalization a win-win option? The same study suggests that formalization should yield a net gain to all players in the long run, providing that the appropriate reforms are put in place. It is estimated that the proposed reforms would reduce the cost of establishing and operating businesses by 90 percent, access to mortgage by 91 percent, and enforcement of pledges by 77 percent. Formalization under the given reform measures would benefit the consumer because it would result in additional income per capita after tax of LE 9,400 per year.[6] This amount is equivalent to 1.5 times per capita income in 2002. At the firm level, the average worker's pay package (including social security) would rise LE 46,100. The government would earn an additional LE 93,000 from value added tax. Consumers would be worse off by 1.7 percent of GDP, but the loss would be mitigated by the benefits from improved product quality and of being either workers or entrepreneurs. The cost of formalization to taxpayers is estimated at no more than 0.04 percent of GDP. Aggregated across all firms, formalization could be expected to generate an annual increase in GDP of LE 8.6 billion over 10 years, or 1.3 percent of GDP annually (Galal 2004).

Viewed in this way, formalization represents a win-win situation. This complies with the argument raised by the ILO that there is a desire among informal entrepreneurs to formalize their operations whenever possible because that qualifies them for institutional support denied otherwise (ILO 1991). It also suggests that the progressive legalization of the informal sector is crucial for its integration into society.

A third policy choice is to pursue economic policies that expand the activities of the formal economy and increase its capacity to absorb unemployment. Indeed, in the long run, the creation of growth patterns that involve a trajectory of moving from bad to good jobs represents the only means of escaping from the dilemma of informality. Such growth patterns should involve the improvement of the business environment, pursuit of adequate industrial policies, and, most important, the development of human resources.

In the Middle East and North Africa region the informal sector represents both a safety net and a response to overregulation of the formal sector and rigidities in the labor and capital markets. Given the large numbers of entrants into the labor force on the one hand and the current wave of privatization, public employment downsizing, and inadequate skill structures on the other, the region is faced with a huge underemployment and unemployment problem. Because economic policies have failed to generate enough employment for entrants into the labor force, there has been a proliferation of poor-quality informal sector employment, absorbing mostly those who cannot afford to queue for formal jobs. There is no alternative route out of the dilemma of informality other than the forging of growth regimes robust enough to create sufficient formal and good jobs.

## Notes

1. This region is defined following the ILO definitions.
2. Because of the paucity of comparable data sets across different regions, comparisons between the Middle East and North Africa region and others was made possible only by using the data on the informal sector published in ILO's "Women and Men in the Informal Sector: A Statistical Picture," 2002b.
3. In Syria, which belongs to the Middle East and North Africa region, participation among women is higher (57 percent), although it remains lower than the participation among men in Syria, which stands at 67 percent.
4. In Syria, this percentage is a little higher at 65 percent.
5. The reliance of developing countries on outsourcing to the informal sector further nuances the relationship between bad jobs and economic growth. It is believed that many of the developing countries that managed to compete in international markets and maintain an expanding share of world trade benefited from price edges stemming from their reliance on the informal sector and outsourcing to the small enterprises.
6. LE is "livre Egyptien" or Egyptian pounds. In 2002 one paid 4.50 LE for 1USD.

## Bibliography

Abdel-Fadil, Mahmoud. 2002. "A Survey of the Basic Features and Problems of the Informal Small and Micro-Enterprises in the Arab Region." Paper prepared for the Forum Euro-Méditerranéen des Instituts Economiques (FEMISE).

Arab Monetary Fund. *Arab Unified Economic Report* (various issues). Abu Dhabi, United Arab Emirates: Arab Monetary Fund.

Bourguignon, François. 2005. "Development Strategies for More and Better Jobs." Paper presented at the conference "Help Wanted: More and Better Jobs in a Globalized Economy," World Bank, Washington, DC, April.

Chen, Martha. 2003. "Rethinking the Informal Economy: In an Era of Global Integration and Labor Market Flexibility." Seminar. New Delhi, New Delhi Seminar No. 531, November; see http://www.india-seminar.com/2003/531.htm.

De Soto, Hernando. 1989. *The Other Path: The Economic Answer to Terrorism.* New York: Perseus Books.

———. 1997. "Dead Capital and the Poor in Egypt." Distinguished Lecture Series No.11, Egyptian Center for Economic Studies, Cairo. December.

———. 2000. *The Mystery of Capital: Why Capitalism Triumphs in the West and Fails Everywhere Else.* New York: Basic Books.

Galal, Ahmed. 2004. "The Economics of Formalization: Potential Winners and Losers from Formalization in Egypt." Working Paper No. 95. Egyptian Center for Economic Studies, Cairo, Egypt.

Girgis, M. 2002. "National Versus Migrant Workers in the GCC." In *Employment Creation and Social Protection in the Middle East and North Africa,* ed. H. Handoussa and Z. Tzannatos. Cairo, Egypt: AUC Press.

Handoussa, H., and G. Potter. 1992, "Egypt Informal Sector: Engine of Growth?" Paper presented at MESA Conference, Portland, OR. October.

ILO (International Labour Organization). 1991. "The Dilemma of the Informal Sector." Report of the Director-General, International Labor Conference, 78th session, Geneva, Switzerland.

———. 2001. "Reducing the Decent Work Deficit—A Global Challenge." Report of the Director-General, International Labor Conference, 89th session, Geneva, Switzerland. June.

———. 2002a. Yearbook of Labor Statistics. Geneva, Switzerland.

———. 2002b. "Women and Men in the Informal Sector: A Statistical Picture." International Labour Office, Geneva, Switzerland.

Maloney, William F. 2004. "Informality Revisited." Policy Research Working Paper No. 2965. World Bank, Washington DC.

Radwan, Samir. 2002. "Employment and Unemployment in Egypt: Conventional Problems, Unconventional Remedies." Working Paper No. 70. Egyptian Center for Economic Studies, Cairo, Egypt.

Trebilcock, Anne. 2005. "Decent Work and the Informal Economy." Discussion Paper No. 2005/04. World Institute for Development Economic Research.

World Bank. 2003a. "Unlocking the Employment Potential in the Middle East and North Africa." Edited draft. World Bank, Washington, DC.

———. 2003b and 2005. *World Development Indicators*. Washington, DC: World Bank.

# CHAPTER 4

# Self-Employment: Engine of Growth or Self-Help Safety Net?

## Christopher Woodruff

About one-third of the labor force in low- and middle-income countries is self-employed, and another perhaps 10 to 12 percent is employed as paid or unpaid workers in household enterprises. For decades, self-employment in developing countries was nearly universally viewed as a self-help safety net in economies lacking government-sponsored safety nets. This view began to change with the highly influential book by Hernando de Soto (1989), who proposed a more dynamic view of the sector. De Soto saw household enterprises as the creations of real entrepreneurs prevented by actions of their governments from growing. It is not hyperbole to say that De Soto's *The Other Path* has had a greater influence on the World Bank's private sector agenda than any publication in the past half century. Unshackling the microentrepreneurs by removing government-imposed barriers to registration of businesses and to the hiring of labor is now central in the Bank's agenda.

But how dynamic is the sector? When the barriers are removed, will the household enterprises grow and flourish? Here it is argued that that is a very unlikely outcome. The evidence suggests that microenterprises are unlikely to become powerful engines of growth for the overall economy, even if government barriers to entrepreneurship are removed.

This does not, however, imply that the sector should be ignored. Rather, attention should shift to the power of microenterprises to reduce poverty, and the capacity of the sector to serve as a self-help safety net in low- and middle-income countries.

Given the proportion of developing country labor forces employed in household enterprises, there is surprisingly little evidence on their dynamics. Mead and Liedholm (1998) and Liedholm and Mead (1999) report on the results of either panel or retrospective surveys of microenterprises in several African and Caribbean countries. Their data suggest that birth and death rates of enterprises are very high. Moreover, expansion of employment by existing firms is quite high, about 15 percent per year. However, Mead and Liedholm note that fewer than one-quarter of firms show any growth at all.[1] As discussed below, evidence from more frequent household surveys suggests that the self-employed often grow and then shrink. Observing a change across any two points in time may provide a misleading picture of the sustained growth of microenterprises.

This chapter first reviews evidence that can be read as showing the microenterprise sector's lack of dynamism, suggesting that we should be suspicious of results from short panels that show high rates of growth. The first piece of evidence is simply the cross-country correlation between self-employment and income, which shows a very strong negative correlation between the two. Data from Mexican employment surveys are used to examine differences between individuals who are self-employed working alone, those who hire unpaid family members, and those who hire paid wage workers. This distinction is important because long-term dynamism depends on the ability to hire and manage employees contracted at arm's length. We will see that the firms doing this are both a minority of household enterprises and different in character from other microenterprises.

Next, the chapter turns to evidence on the ability to raise incomes of the self-employed. Here there is much more reason for optimism. Some evidence on returns to capital among microenterprises in Mexico is discussed, and evidence from a five-quarter panel of microenterprises in Sri Lanka is presented. The Sri Lankan panel is unique in that the firms were subject to random capital injections after the first and third waves of the panel. This allows us to say something about the speed at which they decapitalize these injections, particularly those received early in the panel. There are some caveats to the interpretation of these data, and they are discussed later in the chapter.

## Evidence Against Dynamism

The model that best describes entry into self-employment derives from Lucas's seminal 1978 paper. Workers are endowed with some innate entrepreneurial ability. Those above some endogenously determined entrepreneurial ability level will enter self-employment; those above some higher threshold will hire employees. The demand for employees will determine the wage rate in the economy. The wage rate in turn will determine the ability level of the marginal entrepreneur—the individual who is just indifferent between self-employment and wage work.

As Lucas points out, a prediction of the model is that the percentage of the workforce that is self-employed will decrease as an economy's income level rises. Rising income is associated with higher wages. An increase in wages induces the marginal self-employed worker to leave self-employment in favor of wage work. Gollin (2002) uses ILO data to show that this pattern very clearly holds in cross-country data. Although about one-third of the workforce is self-employed in countries with gross domestic product (GDP) per capita of less than $4,000, the percentage falls to about 10 percent in economies with GDP per capita in the $10,000 range. At the aggregate level, we should expect the share of self-employed to fall as economies develop, and we should welcome the implied loss of entrepreneurship.

Of course, some entrepreneurs have to exhibit dynamism for this process to play out. That is, wages will increase only if the demand for labor increases because firms are growing. But which firms will grow, and what are the relevant constraints preventing them from growing sooner or faster? Here the available data are scarcer than we might like. But the Mexican urban employment and microenterprise surveys are used to argue that the relevant constraint is the ability to manage workers contracted at arm's length and that the lack of this ability is the major constraint to growth of household enterprises. The argument is pushed further than the existing data allow, in large part because the literature has arguably focused too much attention on finance and regulation as constraints to growth.

## Two Groups of Microentrepreneurs

In Mexico, and certainly in most countries with a large informal sector, the majority of the self-employed hire no employees. In urban Mexico, represented by the National Urban Employment Survey, about 22 percent of the working population 18 to 65 years of age is self-employed. Of these, just over 60 percent have no employees. Among those hiring workers, about 60 percent hire at least one paid worker.[2] Rates of self-employment are particularly high in retail trade (37 percent of those employed), repair services (48 percent), personal services (31 percent), and construction (28 percent), and low in professional services (13 percent) and manufacturing (11 percent).[3]

Who selects into self-employment? Across all sectors, males are some-what more likely than females to enter self-employment: 24 percent of males and 18 percent of females are self-employed. Self-employment increases with age but decreases with education. Both the age and education relationships are similar in the United States (using 2000 population census data), although the effect of both, and especially the effect of education, is much more pronounced in Mexico.

The relationship between education and self-employment is worth examining further. Table 4.1 shows the results of cross-section regressions on self-employment. The results are from probits in which the dependent variable takes a value of one if an individual is self-employed and zero otherwise. The data are from the second quarter of 2000, but the results are not particularly sensitive to the particular quarter or quarters chosen. The sample is limited to individuals 18 to 65 years of age working one or more hours in the week before the survey. The sample is split into males and females, and observations are weighted by the expansion factors to represent the population of the 44 cities from which the sample was drawn. Education is measured with a series of dummy variables indicating 1–5, 6, 7–8, 9, 10–11, 12, 13–15, 16, and more than 16 years of schooling (no schooling is the base group). Age is measured by 5-year cohort dummies.

The regressions show that for both males and females, self-employment rates increase with age and decrease with education. The remaining regressions on tables 4.1A and 4.1B split the sample into four parts: the self-employed working alone, the self-employed hiring only unpaid family members, the self-employed who hire paid employees, and (for males) the self-employed who have more than 10 employees. There is a notable difference in the effect of education on the probability of being self-employed as defined by working alone or only with unpaid family members on the one hand, and being an employer of paid workers on the other hand. Among those who work alone, and among those employing only unpaid family members, self-employment decreases with education. But among those hiring wage workers, self-employment

**Table 4.1A. Probability of Being Self-Employed, Males**

| | 1 | 2 | 3 | 4 | 5 |
|---|---|---|---|---|---|
| | All self-employed | Own account | Hiring only unpaid family | Hiring paid workers | >10 hiring paid workers |
| Intercept | −1.193*** | −1.226*** | −2.646*** | −2.601*** | −3.922*** |
| | (0.06) | (0.07) | (0.11) | (0.09) | (0.19) |
| 1–5 years schooling | −0.068 | −0.135** | 0.053 | 0.077 | 0.468*** |
| | (0.06) | (0.06) | (0.09) | (0.08) | (0.12) |
| 6 years schooling | −0.164*** | −0.251*** | −0.023 | 0.120 | 0.728*** |
| | (0.05) | (0.06) | (0.09) | (0.08) | (0.13) |
| 7–8 years schooling | −0.111 | −0.190*** | −0.062 | 0.171** | 0.781*** |
| | (0.06) | (0.07) | (0.11) | (0.10) | (0.18) |
| 9 years schooling | −0.275* | −0.369* | −0.194** | 0.144** | 0.821*** |
| | (0.06) | (0.06) | (0.09) | (0.08) | (0.13) |
| 10–11 years schooling | −0.238*** | −0.371*** | −0.129 | 0.216** | 0.922*** |
| | (0.06) | (0.07) | (0.11) | (0.09) | (0.15) |
| 12 years schooling | −0.273*** | −0.427*** | −0.227** | 0.311*** | 1.160*** |
| | (0.06) | (0.06) | (0.09) | (0.08) | (0.13) |
| 13–15 years schooling | −0.234*** | −0.417*** | −0.235** | 0.353*** | 1.277*** |
| | (0.06) | (0.07) | (0.11) | (0.09) | (0.14) |
| 16 years schooling | −0.240*** | −0.578*** | −0.495*** | 0.580*** | 1.650*** |
| | (0.06) | (0.06) | (0.09) | (0.08) | (0.12) |
| >16 years schooling | −0.477*** | −0.905*** | −1.305*** | 0.529*** | 1.488*** |
| | (0.09) | (0.12) | (0.15) | (0.11) | (0.16) |
| 23–27 years of age | 0.326*** | 0.264*** | 0.40*** | 0.363*** | 0.109 |
| | (0.04) | (0.05) | (0.09) | (0.07) | (0.17) |
| 28–32 years of age | 0.588*** | 0.449*** | 0.652*** | 0.670*** | 0.426*** |
| | (0.04) | (0.04) | (0.09) | (0.07) | (0.16) |
| 33–37 years of age | 0.742*** | 0.536*** | 0.812*** | 0.821*** | 0.546*** |
| | (0.04) | (0.04) | (0.08) | (0.07) | (0.16) |
| 38–42 years of age | 0.834*** | 0.559*** | 0.913*** | 0.962*** | 0.679*** |
| | (0.04) | (0.05) | (0.08) | (0.07) | (0.16) |
| 43–47 years of age | 0.988*** | 0.674*** | 1.020*** | 1.102*** | 0.935*** |
| | (0.04) | (0.05) | (0.08) | (0.07) | (0.16) |
| 48–52 years of age | 1.031*** | 0.672*** | 1.161*** | 1.116*** | 0.948*** |
| | (0.04) | (0.05) | (0.09) | (0.07) | (0.16) |
| 53–57 years of age | 1.131*** | 0.723*** | 1.199*** | 1.20*** | 1.040*** |
| | (0.05) | (0.05) | (0.09) | (0.08) | (0.17) |
| 58–65 years of age | 1.203*** | 0.875*** | 1.088*** | 1.149*** | 1.185*** |
| | (0.05) | (0.05) | (0.09) | (0.08) | (0.18) |
| R-sq | 0.061 | 0.04 | 0.076 | 0.074 | 0.146 |
| Number of observations | 102,248 | 102,248 | 102,248 | 102,248 | 102,248 |

*Source:* Author's calculation from 2nd quarter 2000 ENEU data.

***: significant at the 1 percent level; **: significant at the 5 percent level; *: significant at the 10 percent level.

**Table 4.1B. Probability of Being Self-Employed, Females**

| | 1<br>All self-<br>employed | 2<br>Own<br>account | 3<br>Only unpaid<br>family | 4<br>W/wage<br>workers |
|---|---|---|---|---|
| Intercept | −1.301*** | −1.405*** | −2.349*** | −3.288*** |
| | (0.08) | (0.08) | (0.16) | (0.22) |
| 1–5 years schooling | −0.150** | −0.153** | −0.108 | 0.29 |
| | (0.07) | (0.07) | (0.11) | (0.19) |
| 6 years schooling | −0.287*** | −0.308*** | −0.241** | 0.489*** |
| | (0.07) | (0.07) | (0.10) | (0.19) |
| 7–8 years schooling | −0.205** | −0.221** | −0.401*** | 0.692*** |
| | (0.09) | (0.10) | (0.14) | (0.24) |
| 9 years schooling | −0.446*** | −0.469*** | −0.365*** | 0.547*** |
| | (0.07) | (0.07) | (0.11) | (0.18) |
| 10–11 years schooling | −0.384*** | −0.499*** | −0.539*** | 0.872*** |
| | (0.08) | (0.09) | (0.13) | (0.20) |
| 12 years schooling | −0.638*** | −0.685*** | −0.620*** | 0.658*** |
| | (0.07) | (0.07) | (0.11) | (0.18) |
| 13–15 years schooling | −0.666*** | −0.723*** | −0.679*** | 0.601*** |
| | (0.08) | (0.09) | (0.18) | (0.20) |
| 16 years schooling | −0.728*** | −0.846*** | −1.015*** | 0.803*** |
| | (0.07) | (0.07) | (0.14) | (0.18) |
| >16 years schooling | −0.741*** | −0.908*** | 0.997*** | |
| | (0.14) | (0.17) | (0.23) | |
| 23–27 years of age | 0.497*** | 0.510*** | 0.293 | 0.243 |
| | (0.06) | (0.06) | (0.16) | (0.15) |
| 28–32 years of age | 0.808*** | 0.756*** | 0.507*** | 0.684*** |
| | (0.06) | (0.06) | (0.15) | (0.15) |
| 33–37 years of age | 0.90*** | 0.835*** | 0.783*** | 0.684*** |
| | (0.06) | (0.06) | (0.14) | (0.15) |
| 38–42 years of age | 0.969*** | 0.796*** | 0.976*** | 0.867*** |
| | (0.06) | (0.06) | (0.14) | (0.15) |
| 43–47 years of age | 1.077*** | 0.977*** | 0.965*** | 0.803*** |
| | (0.06) | (0.07) | (0.15) | (0.15) |
| 48–52 years of age | 1.175*** | 0.994*** | 1.033*** | 1.005*** |
| | (0.06) | (0.07) | (0.15) | (0.16) |
| 53–57 years of age | 1.310*** | 1.089*** | 1.166*** | 1.028*** |
| | (0.07) | (0.08) | (0.15) | (0.16) |
| 58–65 years of age | 1.429*** | 1.203*** | 0.967*** | 1.308*** |
| | (0.08) | (0.08) | (0.16) | (0.17) |
| R-sq | 0.094 | 0.084 | 0.113 | 0.061 |
| Number of observations | 60,541 | 60,541 | 59,883 | 60,541 |

*Source:* Author's calculation from 2nd quarter 2000 ENEU data.
***: significant at the 1 percent level; **: significant at the 5 percent level.

increases with education. The education gradient is much steeper for larger employers—those with 10 or more workers—than for smaller employers.

Indeed, the relationship between owners' education and the size of firms is evident even in the raw numbers. Among the self-employed working alone, 66 percent (70 percent) of males (females) have 9 years or less of schooling. Among males (females) with 1 to 4 workers, at least one of whom is paid, 43 percent (40 percent) have 9 years of schooling or less. But among those with more than 10 employees, only 20 percent (29 percent) of males (females) have 9 years of schooling or less. These differences occur within, rather than across, sectors. Both the regressions and the raw data are similar for sectors such as retail trade and personal services.

A note of caution on the interpretation of these results is warranted. The comparisons do not necessarily imply that education is the factor determining the growth of firms. Educational outcomes may be determined by other factors that also determine firm size. For example, individuals whose parents are richer may obtain higher levels of education, have more access to financial capital, and have better social connections to both trading partners and government agencies. But the differences between measured attributes associated with own account workers on the one hand, and employers (and especially larger employers) on the other, suggest that movement across these two groups is not likely to be fluid.

Indeed, the differences in selection into the own account (one-person entrepreneurial endeavors) and employer groups are there even when we control for factors such as parental education and income level. A supplemental survey was applied to the Mexican Urban Employment Survey (ENEU for its Spanish initials) during the third calendar quarter of 1994 in seven cities. The supplemental survey provides information on the parents of the adults in the households. Table 4.2 displays results from a multinomial logit with the form of employment on the left-hand side and parent's education[4] and occupation included as right-hand-side variables. Parent's occupation was measured when the individual was 14 years of age. The individual's employment attachment is categorized as follows: wage work, working alone, working only with unpaid family members, having 1 to 4 paid employees, 5 to 9 paid employees, and 10 to 14 paid employees.

Own education has a similar effect in table 4.2 as it does in table 4.1. Two conclusions emerge from the results on parental characteristics in table 4.2. First, individuals whose parent worked alone are themselves more likely to be self-employed, but self-employed without paid employees.

**Table 4.2. Multinomial Logit Results, Males**

|  | Own account | Only unpaid family | W/1–4 wage workers | W/5–9 wage workers | W/10+ wage workers |
|---|---|---|---|---|---|
| Years of schooling | −0.058*** (0.010) | −0.028 (0.016) | 0.030** (0.014) | 0.154*** (0.037) | 0.140*** (0.035) |
| Parent's years schooling | 0.010 (0.012) | −0.018 (0.020) | 0.026 (0.016) | 0.051 (0.033) | 0.061** (0.029) |
| Parent's occupational income | 0.137 (0.140) | 0.059 (0.219) | 0.377** (0.175) | 0.740** (0.335) | 1.100*** (0.289) |
| Parent self-employed | 0.433*** (0.081) | 0.756*** (0.127) | 0.587*** (0.126) | 0.790** (0.322) | −0.311 (0.370) |
| Parent was employer | 0.067 (0.168) | 0.633*** (0.233) | 1.195 (1.606) | 1.710*** (0.323) | 1.714*** (0.269) |
| Number of observations | 7,264 | | | | |
| Pseudo R-square | 0.101 | | | | |

*Source:* Author's calculation from 3rd quarter 1994 ENEU.
*Note:* The base group consists of wage workers.
***: significant at the 1 percent level; **: significant at the 5 percent level.

Those whose parents were employers, on the other hand, are more likely to be employers hiring 5 or more workers. As in the United States and Europe, parental occupation has an impact on occupation in Mexico. Parents reproduce themselves: own account workers beget own account workers or employers with 1–4 workers; employers beget employers. Second, individuals whose parents were engaged in higher-income occupations are more likely to be employers but not more likely to be own account workers.

These data suggest that the self-employed who work alone or with unpaid family members are distinct from those who hire paid employees. The former account for about 70 percent of the self-employed in Mexico. The differences in characteristics suggest differences beyond access to finance and regulation affecting the growth prospects of microenterprises.

These data present a picture that appears to be at odds with the data from Mead and Liedholm (1998) discussed in the introduction to this chapter and with more recent work by Faznyzlber, Maloney, and Rojas (2005). The latter use data from Mexico to show that there is substantial mobility between wage work and self-employment and between own account workers and employer status. Why the difference? First, without doubt there is likely to be growth in some of the microenterprises across time. Ideally, we would have panels along the lines of the United States National Longitudinal Survey of Youth to track individuals across time, but it appears that there are no such panels for low- and middle-income countries. In the short panels we do have, we observe a great deal of movement back and forth between firm sizes and between wage work and self-employment. The Mexican labor survey data allow for the tracking of individuals for five quarters. In any given period, a substantial number of individuals move from wage work to self-employment and vice versa. But about 75 percent of the movement appears to be attributable to "highly mobile" individuals, those who move more than once during five quarters.[5]

There is similar back-and-forth movement with respect to firm size. For example, among the 2,393 own-account males entering the ENEU sample in the first quarter of 1999, about 15 percent—364—became employers in the second quarter of 1999. But only 63 of these reported being employers in each of the three quarters they remained in the survey. Moreover, of these 63, only 40 hire wage workers and only 3 reported hiring 5 or more workers three quarters later in their final survey. So although there appears to be substantial mobility between any two points in time, it is unclear how much of this mobility could be said to support a view that the sector is dynamic. In any case, we are not likely to obtain agreement on this without data covering a longer period of time.

## Evidence that Incomes Can Be Increased

A significant part of the self-employed work with an extremely small amount of capital. In Mexico in 1998, for example, among males working 35 hours or more per week, 25 percent have $135 or less in invested capital, measured at replacement cost, and half had $950 or less. Among firms with less than the median level of capital invested, reported earnings were $172 per month. Can their incomes be raised? Here the data from Mexico and from a project in Sri Lanka suggest the answer is yes. McKenzie and Woodruff (2006) use data from the Mexican Microenterprise Survey to estimate returns to capital in microenterprises. They find that marginal returns are highest in the very smallest firms—those reporting less than $500 in invested capital, measured at replacement cost.

Figure 4.1 reproduces graphs on returns to capital from McKenzie and Woodruff (2006). They find that marginal returns to capital are extremely high among firms with less than $200 of invested capital, and high among firms with less than $1,000 invested.[6] Taken at face value, these data suggest that allowing the smallest firms to grow will generate higher incomes.

**Figure 4.1. Returns to Capital with Controls, All Industries**

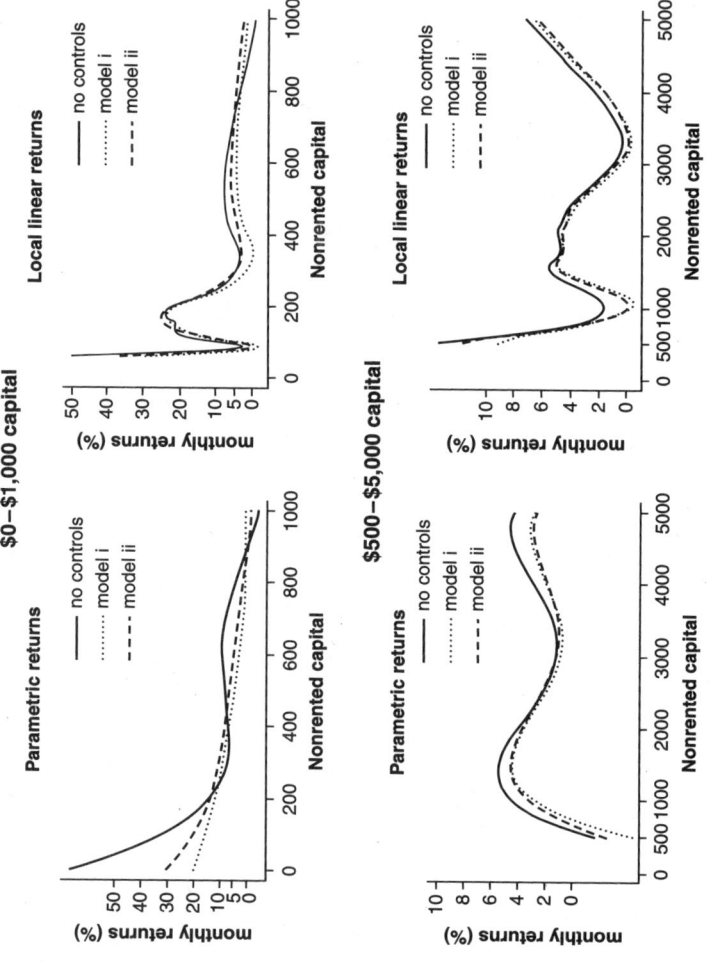

*Source:* McKenzie and Woodruff 2006.

An ongoing project in Sri Lanka is designed to test the hypothesis on the effect of increased capital on the operation of businesses suggested by McKenzie and Woodruff (2006).[7] A survey was done by de Mel, McKenzie, and Woodruff of 600 microenterprises with no more than $1,000 in capital invested in assets other than land and buildings. The firms were selected with a screening survey administered at the household level in three provinces in southern Sri Lanka. An equal number of firms were sampled in each of three zones. The first zone was near the coast, in an area flooded by the December 2006 tsunami. The second zone was in an area immediately inland from the affected zone. Firms in this zone suffered no direct damage from the tsunami, but the demand for their products was affected by the tsunami. The third zone was farther inland in an area in which there was neither direct damage nor a large effect on demand. For the data presented here, the firms in the directly affected zone are eliminated, but note that for the effects examined here, the results are qualitatively similar whether all three zones are used or whether the third zone is used by itself.

The first survey was administered in April 2005 and, to date, the firms have been surveyed quarterly a total of five times. The basic survey instrument is similar to Mexico's National Survey of Microenterprises (ENAMIN by its Spanish initials). Firms are asked both about investments and about current expenditures and revenues. The project also included a series of random capital shocks for the firms. After the first survey in April, we randomly selected 216 of the 600 firms to receive either a cash award or equipment for their enterprise. One-third of the selected firms (or 72 firms) received 10,000 Sri Lankan rupees (about $100) in cash, 72 firms received 10,000 rupees in equipment for their enterprise, 36 firms received 20,000 rupees in cash, and the remaining 36 received 20,000 rupees in equipment. For equipment awards, research assistants working for the project went with the entrepreneurs to purchase the tools, machinery, or inventories selected by the entrepreneurs. The intention was that they purchase the items they felt were most valuable to the enterprise.

Random capital shocks from round 1 provide evidence on two questions.[8] First, how much of the capital invested in the firms remains two, three, and four quarters later? Second, how much do sales change in the quarters following the capital shocks? Table 4.3 shows the effect of the treatments on the investment levels in the firms. Both the mean and the medians of the data are shown. Using either, the treatments have a clear effect on the amount of capital invested in assets other than land and buildings. The treated firms have investment levels that are 105.6 percent of the untreated firms in the baseline (table 4.3A). But in round 2, the gap widens, with the treated firms' investment levels reaching 135.4 percent of the untreated firms investment levels. By round 5 of the survey, almost a year after the treatments, the gap has fallen back somewhat, to 121 percent. The initial impact is smaller at the median, 110 percent, and increases to 123 percent after round 3 before falling very slightly to 119 percent after round 5.

A similar pattern emerges when we focus on inventory investment. Baseline inventory levels are almost identical (table 4.3B). After the treatment, inventory levels among the treated firms increase to 136 percent (200 percent) at the mean (median), after which the gap declines to 109 percent (117 percent) by round 5. The pattern is also similar for revenues—the capital shocks result in the treated firms having revenues 143 percent at the mean, or 141 percent at the median, of untreated

**Table 4.3A. Effect of Treatments on Investment Levels, Total Nonland Capital**

|  | Mar 05 | Jun 05 | Sep 05 | Dec 05 | Apr 06 |
|---|---|---|---|---|---|
| Untreated firms |  |  |  |  |  |
| Mean | 27,280 | 31,387 | 32,652 | 33,700 | 34,812 |
| Median | 20,000 | 25,225 | 25,750 | 26,505 | 24,275 |
| Treated firms |  |  |  |  |  |
| Mean | 28,813 | 42,509 | 40,270 | 41,454 | 42,229 |
| Median | 22,010 | 27,610 | 31,600 | 30,000 | 28,910 |
| Treated/untreated |  |  |  |  |  |
| Mean | 105.6% | 135.4% | 123.3% | 123.0% | 121.3% |
| Median | 110.1% | 109.5% | 122.7% | 113.2% | 119.1% |

*Source:* Author's calculation.

**Table 4.3B. Effect of Treatments on Investment Levels, Inventory Levels**

|  | Mar 05 | Jun 05 | Sep 05 | Dec 05 | Apr 06 |
|---|---|---|---|---|---|
| Untreated firms |  |  |  |  |  |
| Mean | 13,814 | 16,470 | 17,094 | 17,639 | 18,229 |
| Median | 5,000 | 5,000 | 6,000 | 6,900 | 6,000 |
| Treated firms |  |  |  |  |  |
| Mean | 13,805 | 22,426 | 19,258 | 19,060 | 19,925 |
| Median | 5,000 | 10,000 | 8,000 | 8,500 | 7,000 |
| Treated/untreated |  |  |  |  |  |
| Mean | 99.9% | 136.2% | 112.7% | 112.3% | 109.3% |
| Median | 100.0% | 200.0% | 133.3% | 123.2% | 116.7% |

*Source:* Author's calculation.

**Table 4.3C. Effect of Treatments on Investment Levels, Revenues**

|  | Mar 05 | Jun 05 | Sep 05 | Dec 05 | Apr 06 |
|---|---|---|---|---|---|
| Untreated firms |  |  |  |  |  |
| Mean | 13,336 | 16,721 | 19,511 | 21,291 | 22,201 |
| Median | 8,000 | 8,500 | 10,000 | 10,000 | 12,500 |
| Treated firms |  |  |  |  |  |
| Mean | 12,649 | 23,859 | 25,367 | 28,584 | 30,749 |
| Median | 7,000 | 12,000 | 12,000 | 15,000 | 15,000 |
| Treated/untreated |  |  |  |  |  |
| Mean | 94.8% | 142.7% | 130.0% | 134.3% | 138.5% |
| Median | 87.5% | 141.2% | 120.0% | 150.0% | 120.0% |

Source: Author's calculation.

**Table 4.3D. Effect of Treatments on Investment Levels, Profits**

|  | Mar 05 | Jun 05 | Sep 05 | Dec 05 | Apr 06 |
|---|---|---|---|---|---|
| Untreated firms |  |  |  |  |  |
| Mean | 3,794 | 4,313 | 5,964 | 5,394 | 7,768 |
| Median | 3,000 | 3,000 | 3,750 | 4,000 | 5,000 |
| Treated firms |  |  |  |  |  |
| Mean | 3,936 | 5,340 | 5,530 | 5,575 | 9,934 |
| Median | 3,000 | 4,000 | 4,500 | 4,600 | 5,000 |
| Treated/untreated |  |  |  |  |  |
| Mean | 103.7% | 123.8% | 92.7% | 103.4% | 127.9% |
| Median | 100.0% | 133.3% | 120.0% | 115.0% | 100.0% |

Source: Author's calculation.

firms in round 2 (table 4.3C). The gap at the mean remains almost unchanged, being 139 percent in round 5, whereas the gap at the median falls somewhat to 120 percent. Finally, the data for profit levels are somewhat more muddled (table 4.3D). The treatment has an apparent impact in round 2 on both the mean and median profit levels, with profits increasing to 124 percent of the untreated group level at the mean and 133 percent at the median. By round 5, the median profit levels are identical; the mean profit level of the treated firms remains 128 percent of the untreated firm level. This may reflect the fact that the smallest firms are decapitalizing more quickly, or it may reflect only the noisiness of reported profit data.

Though very preliminary, these data suggest that additional capital does result in higher revenues for the smallest microenterprises. Moreover, microentrepreneurs appear to leave the capital in the firm for at least some period of time, and the higher investment levels result in both higher sales levels and higher profits, at least for some period of time.

## Conclusions

Household enterprises and microentrepreneurs become much less numerous as economies develop and incomes and wages increase. Some of the very small firms currently operating increase in size, but the vast majority of people working in them become wage workers. There is a clear divide between the characteristics of the self-employed who work by themselves and the self-employed who hire paid wage workers. Those who hire paid workers have higher education levels, are more likely to come from families of business owners, and have parents with both higher education levels and higher incomes. The stark differences between the own-account workers and employers, especially larger employers, makes it unlikely that the typical own-account worker will grow to become an employer. Longer-term panel data that include information on firm size would be helpful to confirm or disprove this.

The analysis of the Mexican data is at odds in some respects with the work from other countries described by Liedholm and Mead. The differences may be explained by differences in the type of survey data used in the analysis. Mead and Liedholm note that somewhat less than a quarter of the firms grow year to year. Consistent with this, we find that about 15 percent of the self-employed in urban Mexico become employers from one calendar quarter to the next. However, the Mexican data indicate that almost all of the enterprises that grow return to their original size in subsequent quarters. We find fewer than 2 in 1,000 self-employed becoming employers of 5 or more workers within a year. Thus, in any cut of the cross section, the data will show a substantial number of firms growing in size. How often that growth is sustained over a longer period of time is an open question that awaits longer-term panels.

Even if the informal sector is best seen as it traditionally has been, as a self-help safety net, recent research indicates why the sector should not be ignored. Marginal capital investments made by microentrepreneurs appear to be quite profitable. The microentrepreneurs making investments in their firms see revenues and profits increase, at least for some period of time after the investment is made. Preliminary analysis from an ongoing project in Sri Lanka indicates that, although incomes rise immediately following capital injections, the higher levels of income are often not sustained even several quarters later. Training or other interventions may need to accompany capital shocks for the benefits to be sustained over longer periods.

## Notes

The author thanks Bill Maloney, Pieter Serneels, and participants of the conference for many useful comments. Remaining errors are the author's responsibility.

1. Bosh and Maloney (2006) and Bosch, Goni, and Maloney (2006) also show high rates of entry and exit in Mexico and Brazil.

2. The focus is on urban areas, for which more data are available. The 1998 National Employment Survey indicates that self-employment accounts for about 34 percent of the workforce in rural areas. A larger percentage of the enterprises have employees (46 percent), but only 30 percent of those with employees have paid employees. The 2000 population census data also indicate that self-employment is higher in rural areas. In both cases, this is largely explained by the high rates of self-employment in agriculture.

3. These percentages are based on the Mexican Urban Employment Survey (ENEU for its Spanish initials) from the second quarter of 2000. Except for the period immediately following the 1994 peso crisis, the percentage of self-employment has not changed substantially over time during the past couple of decades in Mexico. Bosch and Maloney (2006) show the proportion of the workforce that was informal during the 1987–2003 period. Though they differentiate formal and informal by benefits rather than firm size, their data show a similar consistency across time.

4. Information was gathered on the person who was the head of the household at the time the individual was 14 years of age. In about 83 percent of the cases, it was the father.

5. Among males 18 to 65 who entered the survey in the first quarter of 1999, for example, 10 percent switch into or out of self-employment at least once, 11 percent switch twice, 4 percent switch three times, and 1 percent four times.

6. Banerjee and Duflo (2005) review other evidence on returns to capital among micro and small enterprises. There is growing evidence of returns exceeding 70 percent per year among these firms in India and Africa as well as Mexico.

7. The project is being undertaken by Suresh de Mel, David McKenzie, and Christopher Woodruff. The analysis of the data is just under way, but the project will be referred to as de Mel, McKenzie, and Woodruff.

8. After the third survey round in November 2005, a second round of treatments was administered. We selected 134 of the firms not receiving treatments after round 1, and cash and equipment awards of 10,000 and 20,000 rupees were given in the same proportions as those used in the earlier treatments. Those data are not used because we do not yet have enough follow-up surveys to see their effect. Firms in the directly affected zone had a higher probability of receiving a treatment after the first round and a lower probability after the

third round, relative to the other zones. The treatments were structured this way to distribute more money quickly to the directly affected firms.

## References

Banerjee, Abhijit, and Esther Duflo. 2005. "Growth Theory through the Lens of Development Economics." In *Handbook of Economic Growth*, ed. Aghion and Durlauf. Elsevier Press.

Bosch, Mariano, and William F. Maloney. 2006. "Gross Worker Flows in the Presence of Informal Labor Markets. The Mexican Experience 1987–2002." Working paper. World Bank, Washington, DC.

Bosch, Mariano, Edwin Goni, and William F. Maloney. 2006. "The Determinants of Rising Informality in Brazil: Evidence from Gross Worker Flows." Working paper. World Bank, Washington, DC.

De Soto, Hernando. 1989. *The Other Path*. New York: Harper and Row.

Faznyzlber, Pablo, William F. Maloney, and Gabriel Montes Rojas. 2005. "Microfirm Dynamics in Less Developed Countries: How Similar Are They to Those in the Industrialized World? Evidence from Mexico." Working paper. World Bank, Washington, DC.

Gollin, Douglas. 2002. "Getting Income Shares Right." *Journal of Political Economy* 100 (2): 458–74.

Liedholm, Carl, and Donald Mead. 1999. *Small Enterprises and Economic Development: The Dynamics of Micro and Small Enterprises*. New York: Routledge Studies in Development Economics, Routledge.

Lucas, Robert. 1978. "On the Size Distribution of Firms." *Bell Journal of Economics* 9: 508–23.

McKenzie, David, and Christopher Woodruff. 2006. "Do Entry Costs Provide an Empirical Basis for Poverty Traps? Evidence from Mexican Microenterprises." *Economic Development and Cultural Change* 55 (1): 3–42.

Mead, Donald, and Carl Liedholm. 1998. "The Dynamics of Micro and Small Enterprises in Developing Countries." *World Development* 26 (1): 61–74.

# CHAPTER 5

# Poverty and Earnings Mobility in Three African Countries

## Justin Sandefur, Pieter Serneels, and Francis Teal

## Introduction

Understanding the performance of small-scale enterprises is crucial to unraveling the challenge of poverty in Africa. Across the region, evidence from household surveys shows that the largest share of the poor are in the rural sector, which is dominated by very small scale, household-based farming enterprises. However, rural and urban income distributions have a large overlap with a significant share of the poor in urban areas, typically concentrated in petty trading and self-employment activities. Thus a common factor spanning both peasant farming and the urban informal sector is the link between small-scale activities and poverty.

Two broad views on this issue can be identified in the literature. The first is an old idea (Lewis 1954) that has made a recent reappearance (Murphy et al. 1989) and that expects the small-scale sector to disappear with economic development. "Virtually every country that experienced rapid growth of productivity and living standards over the last 200 years has done so by industrializing." These are the opening words of the paper by Murphy et al. (1989), which claims that the transformation of an economy involves a fundamental change in economic structure, such that the scale of organization increases. In poor economies a large share of the population works in small-scale agriculture, and small-scale activities also dominate within the urban sector. Such a proliferation of small-scale activities is seen as a failure of the process of industrialization. Although many possible sources of such failure have been argued for—a failure to internalize externalities, the lack of an entrepreneurial class, the existence of kleptocractic autocrats with no interest in long-run growth, or excessive taxation—all have in common the view that the fate of the small-scale sector is to disappear with successful development.

In contrast, the implicit view in many policy discussions is that because the poor reside in the small-scale sector, policies that are pro-poor must involve raising the incomes in this sector (World Bank 2005). A variant on this second view is that although the rural sector may need to contract, a key part of a successful development path is a rise in its productivity so that labor can be "released" to the more rapidly growing, modern, urban-based sector. This is combined with a focus on promoting small- and medium-scale enterprises in urban sectors because they are perceived to be pro-poor (because they provide jobs and represent activities that can be entered into with very little capital). Promoting such enterprises has been, and remains, a central part of government policies in virtually all poor countries.

Such a characterization of alternative views is inevitably broad brush and cannot do justice to the many nuances and qualifications that are to be found in the literature.[1] However, what appears striking is the lack of evidence on dynamics both within and across sectors. If it is true that small-scale activities are low-income activities, are they undertaken mainly by the young as part of an investment in skills that lead to higher income later? Alternatively, are mainly older workers found there who, due to changes in demand or the opening up of an economy to trade, have lost their wage jobs and are forced into a "sink" sector? Unless we know something about the dynamics of movement, these questions cannot be answered with any certainty.

The first view presented above expects the development process to be dominated by moves across sectors and regions; the second recommends policies to increase earnings within sectors. To empirically investigate either of these processes requires a panel dimension to any data. We need to know who is going where to do what.

This chapter makes use of embryonic labor market panel surveys of the urban sectors of Ghana and Tanzania and a longer-term survey from Ethiopia to address some aspects of the second view. As Kingdon,

Sandefur, and Teal (2005) document, by far the most rapid increase in employment in both Tanzania and Ghana has been in nonrural self-employment. So one important dimension of the income path followed by individuals is when and how they move between waged and self-employment, but the first step is to investigate movements into *any* earning activities. One implication of the Harris-Todaro model is that "unemployment" in the urban sector in Africa is a search phenomenon; those who are classified as unemployed are simply waiting for the higher-earning wage jobs, so the role of unemployment is to establish an equilibrium between the expected wages across the urban and rural sectors. A later section presents the existing evidence on movements both into earning activities and within earning activities between the self-employed and wage earners.

The next section poses two preliminary questions. Is it true that incomes among the self-employed are lower than those of wage employees and, if so, by how much? Is it true in the cross-section that earnings growth through experience and tenure differ across those in self-employment and those in wage employment? At present the only answers to these questions come from the cross-section data, and it is not possible to discern whether the pattern is driven by movement across jobs or changes within jobs. The chapter concludes with a discussion of just how important it is to know which of these processes is driving the substantial earnings growth observed in the cross-section data.

## What Are Earnings in Alternative Jobs?

If movement across activities is an important part of the process of income growth at the individual level, then a necessary prelude to understanding such processes is the need to know incomes in alternative occupations. Most work on incomes has focused on wages since measuring such incomes is relatively straightforward. However, such a restriction makes comparisons across sectors virtually useless because wage employment refers to a far smaller proportion of the workforce than self-employment.

This section sets out earnings functions for Ghana, Tanzania, and Ethiopia for both wage and self-employment. The recorded incomes for wage employees includes an element of the returns to human capital; the self-employed incomes includes the returns to both human and physical capital. As is well known, there is a substantial part of wage dispersion that cannot be explained by observed human capital (Mortensen 2005). How much of this is due to unobservable skills, efficiency wages, rent, risk sharing among firms, or a process of job search with job matching frictions is a major part of the research agenda for empirical labor economics.

From a policy perspective, it matters a great deal which of these factors is the most important in explaining the income dispersion observed between wage earners and the self-employed. If the key is the unobserved skills of the worker, then the education and training that impart those skills become a key policy issue for raising incomes. If it is a process of sorting among firms, in which firm characteristics play a major role in the income determination process, then changes in the industrial structure in the economy will have a direct impact on the process of incomes and their dispersion.

The data for Ghana and Tanzania are from the 2004 and 2005 rounds of the Ghana and Tanzania Household Worker Surveys. Both surveys were based on a representative sample of the working-age (15–60 years) population in major urban areas (for Ghana: Accra, Tema, Kumasi, Takoradi, and Cape Coast; for Tanzania: Dar es Salaam, Tanga, Iringa, Arusha, Mwanza, and Morogoro).[2] For earnings, attention is confined to earnings in the summers of 2004 and 2005.

For Ethiopia, the data are taken from urban labor force surveys for two years—1994 and 2000. The survey instrument in Ethiopia collected self-employment incomes from female-headed households differently from that of own account workers, who are predominantly male (about 70 percent). As will be apparent from the tables, the approach creates a large gender-based differential for the self-employed in Ethiopia. It cannot be known with any certainty how much of the differential is a true gender differential and how much is due to the difference in the survey instrument. This is controlled for by a dummy for female-headed households in the Ethiopian regression. Although the problems this method poses for interpretation are recognized, the purpose in comparing across the three countries is to draw attention to some of the remarkable similarities that appear to exist both across countries and across the wage and self-employment sectors. Indeed, it is part of the purpose of this chapter to argue that the measurement of self-employment incomes is a key task if the poverty implications of changes to the urban labor force in Africa are to be understood.

Tables 5.1 and 5.2 set out the descriptive statistics on which the earnings functions will be based. Table 5.1 provides an overview of the earnings data across the three countries in U.S. dollars. Because the distributions are highly skewed, the focus is on the medians as a better measure of central

**Table 5.1. Earnings by Occupation Category**

|  | Ghana | | Tanzania | | Ethiopia | |
|---|---|---|---|---|---|---|
|  | Mean (s.d.) | Median (n) | Mean (s.d.) | Median (n) | Mean (s.d.) | Median (n) |
| Civil servant | 102 (55) | 96 (75) | 132 (122) | 98 (131) | 62 (40) | 52 (321) |
| Private sector worker | 63 (60) | 46 (303) | 76 (241) | 45 (136) | 46 (41) | 34 (150) |
| Public sector worker | 103 (67) | 95 (43) | 129 (97) | 122 (29) | 56 (45) | 48 (132) |
| Self-employment | 57 (55) | 45 (780) | 78 (303) | 39 (637) | 88 (194) | 22 (188) |

*Source:* Authors' calculation.
*Note:* All earnings are reported in U.S. dollars per month, averaged over all waves of data.

**Table 5.2. Summary Statistics for Regression Sample**

|  | Ghana | Tanzania | Ethiopia |
|---|---|---|---|
| Male | 0.45 (0.50) | 0.46 (0.50) | 0.53 (0.50) |
| Age (yrs) | 34.30 (9.33) | 38.69 (9.98) | 35.76 (9.82) |
| Education (yrs) | 8.64 (4.21) | 8.40 (3.33) | 9.03 (4.61) |
| Tenure (yrs) | 10.45 (9.13) | 10.79 (8.35) | 10.25 (9.03) |
| Firm size | 67.02 (124.46) | 37.64 (93.40) | 91.00 (182.68) |
| Employees | 1.30 (1.07) | 1.28 (0.87) | 3.79 (22.19) |

*Source:* Authors' calculation.
Values reported are the sample means; standard deviations are in parentheses. "Firm size" refers to the employment level in the firm in which a wage employee works (reported only for wage employees). "Employees" refers to the number of workers *employed by* a self-employed individual (reported only for self-employed).

tendency than are the means. The table shows clearly that those working in the public sector, either as civil servants or in public enterprises, earn more than those in the private sector. In Ethiopia, median earnings of private sector workers are two-thirds of those in public enterprises; in Ghana, they are half; and in Tanzania, one-third. In both Ghana and Tanzania there is a remarkable similarity between earnings in private sector wage employment and self-employment; earnings in these occupations are about US$45 per month. Median self-employment earnings in Ethiopia are much lower at US$22 per month, although this may reflect measurement problems from the questionnaire.[3]

Table 5.2 presents the summary statistics on which the regressions in table 5.3 are based. Education is defined as years of education, age is the age of the worker at the time of the interview, and tenure is the length of time in the worker's current "job" in years. For the self-employed the variable "employees" is the number of employees in the enterprise run by the self-employed "owner." For wage workers a dummy is included for whether or not the worker is a manager. The log of firm size is also included.

Using these data, table 5.3 reports earnings functions for both the self-employed and wage earners. In the pooled regressions (columns 1, 4, and 7) a wage dummy is identified for the three categories of wage worker identified in table 5.1. Because the pooled regression also includes the log of firm size, the coefficient on these dummies can be interpreted only conditional on firms of a given size. This is an important point to which this chapter returns when the earnings distributions are discussed.

These cross-sections demonstrate how both human capital characteristics and the nature of the workplace are correlated with earnings. Figure 5.1 shows how earnings vary with age and tenure for the three countries imputed from the results in table 5.3. The shape of the age earnings profile is broadly similar across all the countries and is concave as is found in virtually all such data. What is striking about the age earnings profile for both Ghana and Ethiopia is how steep it is. During the 20 years from 15 to 35, earnings rise by nearly 80 percent in both countries. There is a rise in Tanzania, but it is less steep and less precisely estimated. Figure 5.1 also shows the tenure profile, which is rising during the early part of the working life cycle for all three countries. The figure is confined to the average across both wage earners and the self-employed. What seems striking from table 5.3 is that such steep profiles are not confined to wage earners. Indeed, because the pooled sample is dominated by the self-employed, the age earning profiles shown in figure 5.1 are effectively those of the self-employed. Something is driving up earnings in both wage and self-employment over the age range from 15 to 35, and understanding the source of this rapid growth is key to understanding how much poverty status may decline as an individual acquires more work experience.

The earnings functions also imply that the shape of the earnings-education profile across the wage and self-employed in Ghana and

**Table 5.3. Earnings Functions**

| | Ghana | | | Tanzania | | | Ethiopia | | |
|---|---|---|---|---|---|---|---|---|---|
| | All (1) | Self (2) | Wage (3) | All (4) | Self (5) | Wage (6) | All (7) | Self (8) | Wage (9) |
| Male | 0.305 | 0.397 | 0.178 | 0.343 | 0.399 | 0.253 | 0.298 | 0.478 | 0.285 |
| | (0.049)*** | (0.068)*** | (0.068)*** | (0.068)*** | (0.070)*** | (0.161) | (0.061)*** | (0.356) | (0.045)*** |
| Age | 0.073 | 0.057 | 0.102 | 0.037 | 0.005 | 0.068 | 0.056 | 0.073 | 0.059 |
| | (0.019)*** | (0.026)** | (0.027)*** | (0.03) | (0.028) | (0.056) | (0.034)* | (0.08) | (0.020)*** |
| $Age^2/100$ | -0.092 | -0.077 | -0.122 | -0.048 | -0.001 | -0.091 | -0.05 | -0.042 | -0.066 |
| | (0.026)*** | (0.034)** | (0.037)*** | (0.041) | (0.035) | (0.081) | (0.043) | (0.099) | (0.026)** |
| Educ | -0.048 | -0.039 | 0.004 | -0.01 | 0.014 | 0.014 | 0.044 | 0.21 | -0.05 |
| | (0.015)*** | (0.023)* | (0.024) | (0.032) | (0.033) | (0.065) | (0.038) | (0.102)** | (0.025)** |
| $Educ^2/100$ | 0.464 | 0.32 | 0.283 | 0.551 | 0.271 | 0.606 | 0.314 | -0.604 | 0.777 |
| | (0.096)*** | (0.171)* | (0.125)** | (0.208)*** | (0.21) | (0.403) | (0.199) | (0.677) | (0.132)*** |
| Tenure | 0.024 | 0.026 | 0.016 | -0.024 | -0.021 | -0.037 | 0.035 | 0.038 | 0.025 |
| | (0.007)*** | (0.008)*** | (0.009)* | (0.016) | (0.023) | (0.026) | (0.013)*** | (0.031) | (0.008)*** |
| $Tenure^2/100$ | -0.043 | -0.034 | -0.043 | 0.087 | 0.059 | 0.138 | -0.07 | -0.133 | -0.02 |
| | (0.018)** | (0.018)* | (0.019)** | (0.056) | (0.078) | (0.089) | (0.037)* | (0.083) | (0.024) |
| ln(employees) | 0.229 | 0.217 | | 0.492 | 0.529 | | 0.211 | 0.267 | |
| | (0.072)*** | (0.073)*** | | (0.095)*** | (0.092)*** | | (0.145) | (0.174) | |
| ln(firm size) | 0.172 | | 0.16 | 0.19 | | 0.183 | 0.045 | | 0.041 |
| | (0.020)*** | | (0.020)*** | (0.062)*** | | (0.066)*** | (0.024)* | | (0.024)* |
| Civil servant | 0.577 | | 0.792 | 0.64 | | 1.091 | -0.263 | | 0.192 |
| | (0.086)*** | | (0.111)*** | (0.126)*** | | (0.309)*** | (0.187) | | (0.128) |
| Public enterprise | -0.163 | | 0.056 | -0.327 | | 0.116 | -0.477 | | -0.009 |
| | (0.145) | | (0.118) | (0.495) | | (0.375) | (0.223)** | | (0.07) |

*(continued)*

75

**Table 5.3. Earnings Functions** (*continued*)

| | Ghana | | | Tanzania | | | Ethiopia | | |
|---|---|---|---|---|---|---|---|---|---|
| | All (1) | Self (2) | Wage (3) | All (4) | Self (5) | Wage (6) | All (7) | Self (8) | Wage (9) |
| Private enterprise | -0.282 (0.075)*** | | | -0.584 (0.247)** | | | -0.426 (0.220)* | | |
| Female household enterprise | | | | | | | -1.162 (0.262)*** | -0.992 (0.352)*** | |
| Trend | -0.021 (0.045) | -0.017 (0.06) | 0.002 (0.06) | 0.121 (0.068)* | 0.082 (0.068) | 0.144 (0.153) | -0.006 (0.064) | -0.433 (0.246)* | 0.109 (0.044)** |
| Constant | 51.873 (89.225) | 43.555 (120.077) | 4.044 (121.019) | -238.59 (136.324)* | -159.547 (136.25) | -284.611 (305.889) | -1.288 (0.69)* | -2.369 (1.69) | -1.231 (0.371)*** |
| Observations | 1201 | 780 | 421 | 933 | 637 | 296 | 791 | 188 | 603 |
| R-squared | 0.26 | 0.12 | 0.5 | 0.24 | 0.2 | 0.29 | 0.41 | 0.35 | 0.47 |

*Source:* Authors' calculation.

The dependent variable is the log of monthly earnings, before tax, in real domestic currency. "In(employees)" and "In(firm size)" are defined in the notes for table 5.2. "Employees" takes a value of 1 for those not employing wage labor. Similarly, "firm size" is 1 for the self-employed. "Public enterprise," "civil servant," "private enterprise," and "female household enterprise" are dummy variables taking a value of 1 for individuals employed in that sector. Standard errors are in parentheses.

\* significant at 10%; \*\* significant at 5%; \*\*\* significant at 1%.

**Figure 5.1. Age- and Tenure-Earnings Profiles**

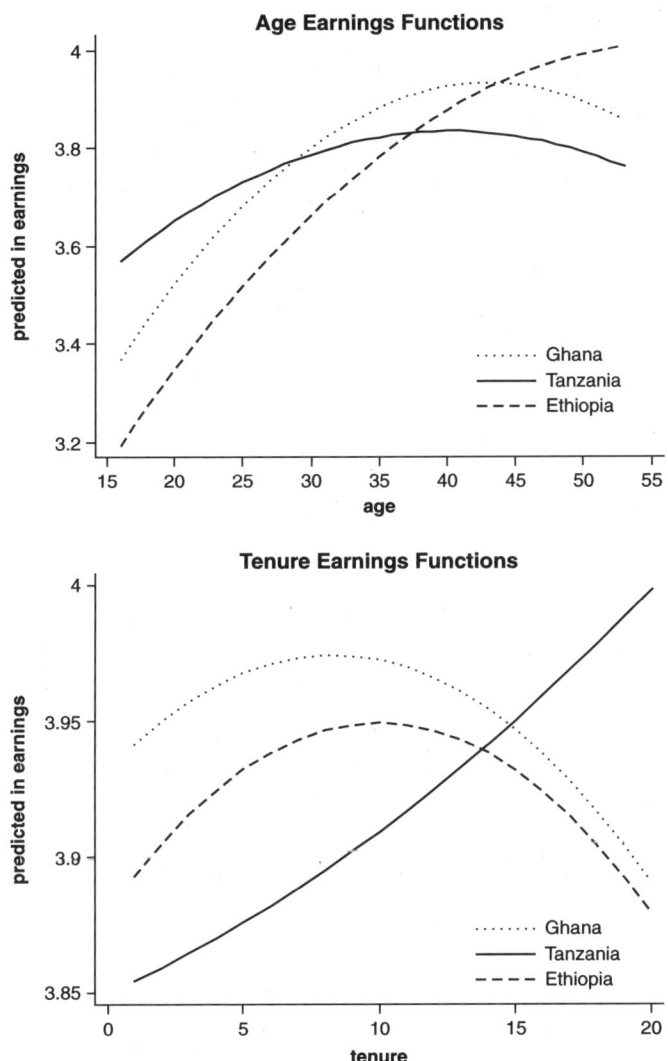

*Source:* Authors' calculation.

Tanzania is similar and that this profile is convex, not concave, in both sectors (see Söderbom et al. 2006 for extensive tests on wage data from firm surveys in Kenya and Tanzania as to whether this convexity can be explained by ability bias). In Ethiopia there is no convexity in the earnings education profile for the self-employed, but this almost certainly reflects the low levels of education in the sector. The median is 4 years, so there are too few observations to pick up the convexity apparent in the other two countries across both wage and self-employment.

As already noted, the pooled regression includes the log of firm size, so the coefficient on the wage dummies can be interpreted only conditional on firms of a given size. For both Ghana and Tanzania the earnings functions imply that the worker in a small firm (one between 5 and 10 employees) has earnings similar to that of a worker who is self-employed—controlling for both education and job tenure. The point estimate on the log of firm size is not only highly significant, it is also large for both countries. The point estimate implies substantial changes in wages as firm size rises. If a worker moves from a firm of 5 employees to one with 100, earnings rise by 62 percent in Ghana and by 71 percent in Tanzania. It is possible that some part of this rise with firm size reflects unobserved skills of the workers. However, in instances in which panel data at the individual level are linked with firm size as in Söderbom, Teal, and Wambugu (2005), the size effect remains large. The measured firm size effect is smaller in Ethiopia, but this may reflect the fact that the measurement of firm size was rather crude in the data.

The results that emerge from the data are clear. Earnings differ little between those in small firms and the self-employed. In the private sector, it is wage earners in large firms who earn substantially more than the self-employed on average. The introduction to this chapter noted that evidence from a broad range of sources suggested that there is a substantial overlap in low incomes across sectors. Figure 5.2 shows the dispersion of earnings across both the self-employed and wage earners; wage earners are divided between those in small firms and those in large firms. For all three countries, the mean earnings for wage employees in small firms and for the self-employed are similar; indeed in Ghana the distributions of the earnings are virtually identical. The picture of an economy in which wage employment offers substantially higher earnings than working in self-employment is only accurate if we confine attention to wage employment in relatively large firms.

Because the regressions use only ordinary least squares (OLS), it is not possible to establish whether the observed processes of rising income are due to learning within a job or are the result of processes of selection by which different "types" of individuals are observed in the labor market at different ages. The next section takes a first step toward answering that question by analyzing the mobility observed within the data.

**Figure 5.2. Individual Income Distributions by Occupation Category**

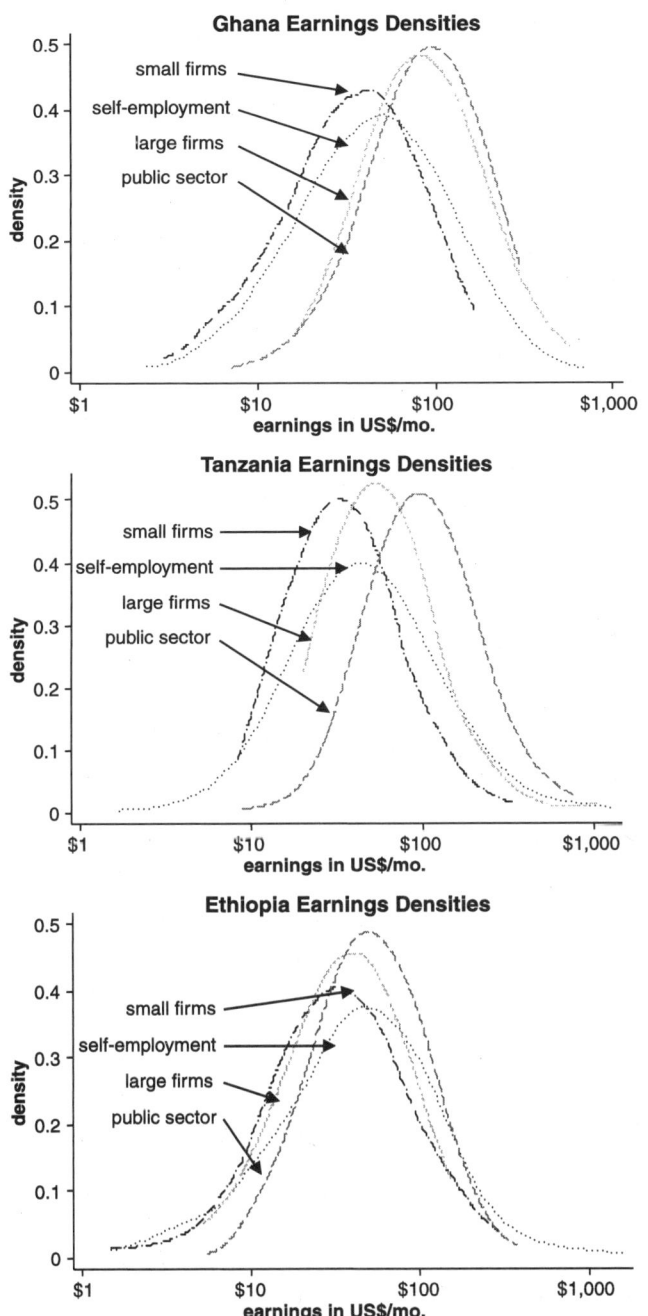

## How Mobile Are Individuals between Different Types of Jobs?

This section draws on the panel dimension of the data to present some preliminary evidence as to how mobile individuals are between jobs. For all three countries the data is confined to the urban sector. Thus the transition matrices presented in figures 5.3–5.5 measure movement during a six-year period for Ethiopia and during one year for Ghana and Tanzania.

The picture presented is sensitive to how transitions are defined. Assumptions made for both Ghana and Tanzania ensure that these transition matrices are *very conservative estimates*—that is, they should be seen as lower bounds on the amount of churning going on in the data. The following rules are adopted:

- Only transitions for workers who reported (in 2005) a job or an unemployment spell that had commenced since their 2004 interview are allowed.
- Numerous respondents who, for instance, described themselves as self-employed in 2004 but as wage employees in 2005 were considered to be in the same job if the reported starting dates indicated these were in fact the same job.
- For individuals who did not report a job commencing since their last interview, their activity in 2005 was forced to correspond to their activity in 2004.

The transitions across the three countries are compared below. The Ghana and Tanzania data have the disadvantages and advantages of an annual panel. The advantage is that it allows measurement of short-term movements and will ensure, if it can be continued, that detailed dynamics can be modeled. However, the disadvantage is that measurement error is likely to be severe.

A major issue in the analysis of labor markets in Africa is the possibility of distinguishing between being unemployed or being out of the labor force. Kingdon, Sandefur, and Teal (2005) show that measured unemployment varies enormously across African economies, with urban Ethiopia and South Africa having some of the highest measured rates in the world; similarly measured unemployment in Tanzania is 1.2 percent and in Ghana 3.5 percent of the labor force. In both Ghana and Tanzania, employment growth has been dominated by the growth of nonrural self-employment, most of which has been in urban areas. The ILO definition of unemployment seeks to make a distinction between having a job and not having one but wanting one (i.e., an unemployed individual is one who does not have a job and is searching for one). In economies experiencing rapid growth in self-employment, the distinction that is being made between having and not having a job breaks down. Jobs are readily available; the issue is not one of being employed or unemployed, it is the incomes available from the self-employed activity and the productivity of such activity.

In his classic discussion of these issues, Sen (1975, p.32) makes a distinction between three approaches to the analysis of nonwage employment:

| | |
|---|---|
| "The production approach: | If this man leaves the family, would the output of the family enterprise go down? |
| The income approach: | Is this man's income (including direct consumption and any other income that he is given) a reward for his work, and will he cease to get it if he stops work? |
| The recognition aspect: | Does he think of himself as "employed"? Do others?" |

These distinctions are useful for the economies for which there are appropriate data. Because this chapter uses only labor force data, the production aspect of employment cannot be measured, but some aspects of the income dimension can. The focus here is on "incomes derived from employment activities," meaning that the activity generates a monetary income. Thus, individuals with no income are defined as inactive (whether or not they are classified as in or out of the labor force) and working as unpaid family labor. This is done to provide the most basic measure of possible transition in the labor market, namely, between having an "income derived from employment activities" and not having one. Moving from "no-income" to "income" is not necessarily an improvement in expenditure for the concerned individual—a young unemployed man living with his family having to move to a new location for work because his family will no longer support him may well experience a fall not rise in expenditure.

### Transition Matrices between "No Income" and "Income"
Figure 5.3 sets out the first set of transition matrices, E1, G1, and T1, which show for Ethiopia, Ghana, and Tanzania, respectively, the movements from "no-income" to having a job (meaning having an "income derived from employment activities"). Recall that the movement for

**Figure 5.3. Transition Matrices between "No income" and "Income"**

**Percentages** | **Absolute Numbers**

**Matrix G1** — Ghana

| | No income | Same job | New job | Total |
|---|---|---|---|---|
| No income | 84 | 0 | 16 | 100 |
| Income | 9 | 85 | 6 | 100 |
| Total | 36 | 54 | 10 | 100 |

| | No income | Same job | New job | Total |
|---|---|---|---|---|
| No income | 277 | 0 | 54 | 331 |
| Income | 50 | 484 | 34 | 568 |
| Total | 331 | 484 | 88 | 899 |

**Matrix T1** — Tanzania

| | No income | Same job | New job | Total |
|---|---|---|---|---|
| No income | 79 | 0 | 21 | 100 |
| Income | 6 | 91 | 3 | 100 |
| Total | 9 | 87 | 4 | 100 |

| | No income | Same job | New job | Total |
|---|---|---|---|---|
| No income | 15 | 0 | 4 | 19 |
| Income | 28 | 431 | 15 | 474 |
| Total | 43 | 431 | 19 | 493 |

**Matrix E1** — Ethiopia

| | No income | Same job | New job | Total |
|---|---|---|---|---|
| No income | 74 | 0 | 26 | 100 |
| Income | 21 | 49 | 30 | 100 |
| Total | 55 | 17 | 27 | 100 |

| | No income | Same job | New job | Total |
|---|---|---|---|---|
| No income | 1,245 | 0 | 430 | 1,675 |
| Income | 189 | 446 | 275 | 910 |
| Total | 1,434 | 446 | 705 | 2,585 |

*Source:* Authors' calculation.

Ethiopia is over a six-year period, whereas for Ghana and Tanzania it is for one year.

This definition shows far more mobility in Ghana and Tanzania than in Ethiopia. In Ghana 16 percent of those with no income in 2004 reported an income in 2005; in contrast, in Ethiopia only 26 percent reported moving to having an income *after six years*.[4] The sample size in Tanzania is very small; since households with no income were undersampled. For this small sample, the figures show higher mobility than in Ghana.

When considering the reverse movements—that is, from income to no-income—similar degrees of mobility across the economies are observed. During the six-year period for Ethiopia, 21 percent moved from income to no-income, and in Ghana and Tanzania the figures were 9 and 6 percent, respectively, during the one year.

### Transition Matrices between "No Income" and "Type of Income"
Figure 5.4 presents a second set of matrices, E2, G2, and T2, in which the focus is on transitions between wage and self-employment. Transitions within wage employment (say from one firm to another) or self-employment (abandoning one business to pursue another) are not recorded here.

For both Ghana and Tanzania there is very little, if any, difference in the degree of mobility for the wage earner and the self-employed. For both types of employment, between 7 and 10 percent change occupation, that is, move out of being either a wage earner or a self-employee. For both countries, most of those who exit wage employment enter the no income category rather than self-employment. A similar pattern exists for the self-employed: those who exit self-employment are far more likely to enter the no-income category than they are to enter wage employment.

The data for Ghana and Tanzania show relatively little movement between wage and self-employment during the one-year period. It is, of course, almost certain that this will change as the panel lengthens. However, little short-term movement between the two sectors is consistent with the finding in the previous section that there is little income difference between those who work in self-employment and those who earn wages in small-scale enterprises. Those who exit from either form of income-earning activity are likely to enter the no-income category, suggesting that they are close to their reservation wages and that individual idiosyncratic factors are sufficient to move them into preferring not to work.

In the case of Ethiopia, there is far more mobility among the self-employed than there is among wage earners. Among those who were self-employed in 1994, 44 percent had moved from being self-employed

# Figure 5.4. Transition Matrices between "No Income" and "Type of Income"

## Percentages

**Matrix G2** Ghana

|  | Wage | App | Self | No inc. | Total |
|---|---|---|---|---|---|
| Wage | 91 | 1 | 2 | 6 | 100 |
| Apprentice | 0 | 90 | 7 | 3 | 100 |
| Self | 2 | 0 | 89 | 9 | 100 |
| No income | 8 | 1 | 10 | 81 | 100 |
| Total | 20 | 5 | 43 | 32 | 100 |

**Matrix T2** Tanzania

|  | Wage | Self | No inc. | Total |
|---|---|---|---|---|
| Wage | 93 | 1 | 6 | 100 |
| Self | 1 | 93 | 6 | 100 |
| No income | 5 | 16 | 79 | 100 |
| Total | 28 | 63 | 9 | 100 |

**Matrix E2** Ethiopia

|  | Wage | Self | No inc. | Total |
|---|---|---|---|---|
| Wage | 77 | 11 | 12 | 100 |
| Self | 12 | 56 | 32 | 100 |
| No income | 12 | 14 | 74 | 100 |
| Total | 23 | 22 | 56 | 100 |

## Absolute Numbers

|  | Wage | App | Self | No inc. | Total |
|---|---|---|---|---|---|
| Wage | 153 | 1 | 3 | 11 | 168 |
| Apprentice | 0 | 38 | 3 | 1 | 42 |
| Self | 6 | 1 | 356 | 37 | 400 |
| No income | 23 | 3 | 28 | 235 | 289 |
| Total | 182 | 43 | 390 | 284 | 899 |

|  | Wage | Self | No inc. | Total |
|---|---|---|---|---|
| Wage | 136 | 2 | 9 | 147 |
| Self | 4 | 304 | 19 | 327 |
| No income | 1 | 3 | 15 | 19 |
| Total | 141 | 309 | 43 | 493 |

|  | Wage | Self | No inc. | Total |
|---|---|---|---|---|
| Wage | 326 | 47 | 51 | 424 |
| Self | 58 | 283 | 160 | 501 |
| No income | 199 | 227 | 1,239 | 1,665 |
| Total | 583 | 557 | 1,450 | 2,590 |

*Source:* Authors' calculation.

by 2000, the majority of those to no-income. For the wage employees, only 23 percent had moved. It is rather striking that during this relatively long period, of those who moved out of self-employment, about 70 percent moved into the no-income category rather than moved into wage employment. For those with a wage job at the beginning of the period, movement out is equally divided between those who entered self-employment and those who entered no-income.

### Transition Matrices between "Labor Force Status" and "Type of Income"

Figure 5.5 presents a third set of matrices, E3, G3, and T3, in which the breakdown of no-income is extended into being out of the labor force (o.l.f.) and unemployed. It is this distinction that is the most problematic for an analysis of labor markets in these economies. The data for Tanzania are reported for completeness, but the undersampling of those unemployed and out of the labor force in the first round of the survey means that the data cannot be used to ask questions relating to movement out of and into either the labor force or unemployment. The focus is therefore on Ethiopia and Ghana.

In Ethiopia, the striking feature of the data is both the high unemployment rate and the large numbers who are classified as being out of the labor force—two facts that are clearly related. Using this classification gives an average unemployment rate of 37 percent. Movement out of unemployment is very slow. Of those unemployed in 1994, only 36 percent had found jobs by 2000, half of these as wage employees and the other half as self-employed.

In Ghana, again accepting the classifications used, the unemployment rate is 20 percent. This is markedly higher than the rates reported in the most recent household survey, which gives an average national figure of less than 4 percent. Mobility here is much higher than in Ethiopia. After one year, 19 percent of the unemployed had moved into a job.

To link these processes of movement to the issues raised in the introduction, both the age and education of those in these occupational categories should be considered—a subject for future work. We also need to ask how much this movement is affecting the interpretation of the earnings set out in the previous section. The next section outlines the importance of these issues for policy questions as to how the rapid changes in occupational structure that are occurring in Africa link to poverty reduction.

# Figure 5.5. Transition Matrices between "Labor Force Status" and "Type of Income"

## Percentages

**Matrix G3**  Ghana

| | Wage | App | Self | o.l.f. | Unemp | Total |
|---|---|---|---|---|---|---|
| Wage | 91 | 1 | 2 | 1 | 6 | 100 |
| Apprentice | 0 | 90 | 7 | 0 | 3 | 100 |
| Self | 1 | 0 | 89 | 1 | 9 | 100 |
| Out of labor force | 9 | 1 | 8 | 74 | 8 | 100 |
| Unemp | 7 | 1 | 11 | 3 | 78 | 100 |
| Total | 20 | 5 | 43 | 12 | 20 | 100 |

**Matrix T3**  Tanzania

| | Wage | Self | o.l.f. | Unemp | Total |
|---|---|---|---|---|---|
| Wage | 93 | 1 | 4 | 2 | 100 |
| Self | 1 | 93 | 5 | 1 | 100 |
| Out of labor force | 8 | 15 | 77 | 0 | 100 |
| Unemp | 0 | 17 | 0 | 83 | 100 |
| Total | 29 | 63 | 6 | 2 | 100 |

**Matrix E3**  Ethiopia

| | Wage | Self | o.l.f. | Unemp | Total |
|---|---|---|---|---|---|
| Wage | 77 | 11 | 6 | 6 | 100 |
| Self | 12 | 56 | 23 | 9 | 100 |
| Out of labor force | 9 | 11 | 60 | 20 | 100 |
| Unemployed | 18 | 18 | 18 | 46 | 100 |
| Total | 23 | 22 | 35 | 20 | 100 |

## Absolute Numbers

Ghana

| | Wage | App | Self | o.l.f. | Unemp | Total |
|---|---|---|---|---|---|---|
| Wage | 153 | 1 | 3 | 1 | 10 | 168 |
| Apprentice | 0 | 38 | 3 | 0 | 1 | 42 |
| Self | 6 | 1 | 356 | 3 | 34 | 400 |
| Out of labor force | 12 | 2 | 11 | 100 | 11 | 136 |
| Unemp | 11 | 1 | 17 | 5 | 119 | 153 |
| Total | 182 | 43 | 390 | 109 | 175 | 899 |

Tanzania

| | Wage | Self | o.l.f. | Unemp | Total |
|---|---|---|---|---|---|
| Wage | 136 | 2 | 6 | 3 | 147 |
| Self | 4 | 304 | 16 | 3 | 327 |
| Out of labor force | 1 | 2 | 10 | 0 | 13 |
| Unemp | 0 | 1 | 0 | 5 | 6 |
| Total | 141 | 309 | 32 | 11 | 493 |

Ethiopia

| | Wage | Self | o.l.f. | Unemp | Total |
|---|---|---|---|---|---|
| Wage | 326 | 47 | 24 | 27 | 424 |
| Self | 58 | 283 | 117 | 43 | 501 |
| Out of labor force | 101 | 129 | 678 | 221 | 1,129 |
| Unemployed | 98 | 98 | 94 | 246 | 536 |
| Total | 583 | 557 | 94 | 537 | 2,590 |

Source: Authors' calculation.

## What Has Been Learned, and What Do We Need to Know?

As is well known, there are considerable practical difficulties in measuring incomes in poor countries, and part of the research task has been to show that this can be done for both wage earners and the self-employed. This chapter began by showing that it is useful to measure self-employment incomes on an individual basis and to estimate earnings functions that capture the effects of age, education, and job characteristics as determinants of earnings. In Ghana and Tanzania, earnings growth during the working lifetime appears to be as great among the self-employed as it is for wage earners.

How can the type of panel data presented in the previous section provide insights into this growth process and directly link to understanding the process of poverty reduction? Data allowing an assessment of the extent to which poverty has been reduced is now based on measures of household per capita (or per adult equivalent) expenditure. The grounds for using such measures are compelling in light of the difficulties of measuring incomes, especially in the poorest countries and in the poorest areas within such countries—the rural areas. However, such procedures create a gap between the measure of poverty, which is expenditure based, and the determinants of such poverty, which clearly depend on income. As was noted in the introduction to this chapter, by far the most rapid increase in employment in both Tanzania and Ghana has been in nonrural self-employment, and the income implications of this shift are crucial for understanding how this change affects poverty.

Expenditure per capita for households headed by a farmer are the lowest of any of the occupational categories for both Ghana and Tanzania. If we are willing to infer from this knowledge of the expenditure data that incomes in rural areas are lower than in urban sectors, it suggests that a key part of the process by which poverty has declined in these two countries has been the impacts of changes across sectors on raising incomes—an inference that reflects the first of the two views of the development process set out in the introduction to the chapter.

Although this process of a shift to urban occupations has decreased poverty, it has done so very slowly and to a very limited extent. Comparative household expenditure data for Ghana and Tanzania suggest that consumption per capita has been growing at about 10 percent *per decade* during the 1990s (see Owens and Teal [2005]). This compares with figures for China of some 5 percent *per year* during a longer period.

The data employed here provide some possible insights into the source of this divergence. Although incomes in urban areas may be higher than in rural areas, there are very limited gains available from shifting across occupations. The reason for this implied by the data is the lack of growth of jobs in relatively large firms. It is there where the higher income earning opportunities lie. If that is the case, policies to promote small-scale at the expense of larger-scale organizations would deepen, not alleviate, poverty. If poverty is to be tackled effectively, understanding how and why *incomes* differ must be a central part of the policy agenda.

## Notes

This paper draws on data collected by the Centre for the Study of African Economies at Oxford University in collaboration with the Ghana Statistical Office, Accra, and the Tanzanian National Bureau of Statistics, Dar es Salaam, during the period from 2003 to 2005. We are greatly indebted to the staff of these agencies for their assistance in organizing the surveys and in collecting the data. We are also gratefull to Neil Rankin, now at the School of Economic and Business Sciences, University of the Witwatersrand, South Africa, who played a key part in the first rounds of the surveys and Trudy Owens of the University of Nottingham, who was responsible for setting up the work in Tanzania. The surveys have been funded, in part, by the Department for International Development of the UK. Justin Sandefur and Francis Teal are funded by the Economic and Social Research Council of the UK and are members of the Global Poverty Research Group. The Ethiopia data were collected in cooperation with Addis Ababa University and Goteborg University.

1. The contrast between the Lewis view and that implied by the Harris-Todaro model is discussed in detail in Meier and Rauch (2005, pp. 360 ff).

2. Although for both countries recall data were collected about the job histories of the workers interviewed, that job history is not used in this chapter.

3. If female household enterprises (which were administered a separate questionnaire) are removed from the sample, the mean and median of self-employment incomes in Ethiopia are US$146 and US$43, respectively.

4. Some caution is needed with the interpretation of this figure, as it may hide movement into and back out of employment over the 6 years.

## Bibliography

Harris, J., and M. Todaro. 1970. "Migration, Unemployment and Development: A Two-Sector Analysis." *American Economic Review* 60 (1): 126–42.

Kingdon, G., J. Sandefur, and F. Teal. 2005. "Labor Market Flexibility, Wages and Incomes in Sub-Saharan Africa in the 1990s." Oxford Global Poverty Research Group Working Paper 030, Manchester and Oxford.

Lewis, W. A. 1954. "Economic Development with Unlimited Supplies of Labour." *The Manchester School* 22: 141–5.

Meier, G. M., and J. E. Rauch. 2005. *Leading Issues in Economic Development*, 8th ed. Oxford, UK: Oxford University Press.

Mortensen, D. T. 2005. *Wage Dispersion: Why Are Similar Workers Paid Differently?* Cambridge, MA: MIT Press.

Murphy, K., A. Shleifer, and R. Vishny. 1989. "Industrialisation and the Big Push." *Journal of Political Economy* (October): 1003–26.

Owens, T., and F. Teal. 2005. "Policies Towards Poverty: Ghana and Tanzania in the 1990s." http://www.gprg.org/themes/t1-pov-house-well/pol-pov-ghan-tanz/pol-pov-ghan-tanz-indepth-05.htm.

Sen, A. 1975. *Employment, Technology and Development*. Oxford, UK: Oxford University Press.

Söderbom, M., F. Teal, and A. Wambugu. 2005. "Unobserved Heterogeneity and the Relation between Earnings and Firm Size: Evidence from Two Developing Countries." *Economic Letters* 87: 153–9.

Söderbom, M., F. Teal, A. Wambugu, and G. Kahyarara. 2006. "The Dynamics of Returns to Education in Kenyan and Tanzanian Manufacturing." *Oxford Bulletin of Economics and Statistics* 68 (1): 261–396.

World Bank. 2005. *Pro-Poor Growth in the 1990s: Lessons and Insights from 14 Countries*. Washington, DC: The World Bank on behalf of the Operationalizing Pro-Poor Growth Research Program.

# CHAPTER 6

# Firm Dynamics, Productivity, and Job Growth

## John Haltiwanger

## Introduction

Recent research using establishment- and firm-level data has raised a variety of conceptual and measurement questions about our understanding of aggregate growth. Several key related findings are of interest. First, in a well-functioning market economy, there is large-scale, ongoing reallocation of outputs and inputs across individual producers. An important and fundamental component of this reallocation is the reallocation of jobs and in turn workers. Second, the pace of this reallocation varies over time (both secularly and cyclically) and across sectors. Third, much of this reallocation reflects within- rather than between-sector reallocation, and involves the entry and exit of businesses. Fourth, there are large differences in the levels and the rates of growth of productivity across firms in the same sector. The rapid pace of output and input reallocation and the heterogeneity across businesses in productivity levels and growth rates play an important role in aggregate productivity growth. Indeed, this is the core finding of the recent empirical literature exploring firm-level data.[1]

However, it would be wrong to conclude immediately that economies that exhibit a greater pace of reallocation are inherently more efficient. It would also be wrong to suspect a simple monotonic empirical relationship between the pace of reallocation and economic growth. If nothing else, different economies (across time or countries) may be experiencing different aggregate and structural shocks. Moreover, economies may react differently due to fundamental differences in their market structure and institutions. In that vein, there are many theoretical reasons why one might suspect that the magnitude, or the timing, or the nature of the reallocation process might be inefficient (see, e.g., Caballero and Hammour 2000a, 2000b) as a result of market imperfections and/or inefficient market institutions. Thus, the contribution of reallocation to growth may vary considerably across economies, depending on the nature of the institutions and the market environment.

There are a host of questions that arise in emerging economies. An initial question is whether the contribution of reallocation to productivity growth is likely to be the same in countries trying to "catch-up" with the most advanced economies. One view is that the experimentation and noisy process of technology adoption is likely to be more relevant in economies in which firms are operating on the cutting edge of new technologies. Although that is an empirical question, much of the theoretical literature emphasizes that the sources of noise and churning among businesses quite likely reflect more than just uncertainty about the "engineering" side of technology.[2] Finding the most appropriate product and process mix (including the mix of workers) for a given location and time period is likely to involve uncertainty and errors. It may be that a particular business model works well in one location but not in another, perhaps due to differences in the underlying markets for factors (labor, materials, capital, energy, and so on) or in the institutional environment. Put differently, this perspective on technology suggests that it is not a matter of simply finding and reading the right blueprints for production. As a result, and contrary to the mentioned view, reallocation may be equally relevant to growth in less developed economies.

Another issue raised by Caballero and Hammour (2000a, 2000b) is that the hold-up problem associated with reallocation may also vary in intensity under different institutional settings.[3] Reallocation involves businesses and workers engaging in a variety of relationships with a high degree of specificity. By specificity, we mean that some of the joint value of a relationship is specific to that particular relationship and would be lost if the parties terminated it. The specific investments that firms and workers make in creating jobs and making matches are some of the factors that yield such specificity. The problem with such relationships is that there can be an ex post hold-up problem, and a question that arises is whether the market structure and institutions yield an efficient solution to the hold-up problem.

Caballero and Hammour (2000a, 2000b) argue that various countries and parts of the world have experienced problems in the institutional and market structure that interact with the hold-up problem with significant adverse aggregate consequences. For example, they argue that this is a more severe issue in transition economies because of an under-developed legal and institutional environment, a lack of transparency, and lax corporate governance standards. In Western Europe, hold-up problems are exacerbated by labor market regulation that stifles this reallocation process. In all of these cases, the limitations of the institutional/market structure stifle and distort the ongoing reallocation process (and thus the ability to tap new technological developments, as well as to adapt to a changing environment).

In short, the dynamics of growth, productivity, and reallocation are fundamental issues for all economies but loom particularly large for emerging market economies. Getting all of the pieces in place for a well-functioning market economy (that is, competitive product markets with liberal trade policies, property rights and a well-functioning legal system, well-functioning credit markets, labor market flexibility, and sustainable and sound monetary and fiscal policies) is one of the major challenges such economies face. Restructuring and reallocation are thus crucial for economies trying to make product and factor markets more flexible. The question is, what policies work better in achieving such flexibility in the context of developing countries? Related questions we need to ask are, what are the implications of this flexibility in regard to unemployment and lower wages for workers, and how do the benefits of flexibility balance out against the costs?

An extensive literature has emerged that (i) documents the nature of firm dynamics via the pace of entry and exit and job dynamics; (ii) explores the connection between reallocation and productivity growth; and (iii) explores the role of institutions in accounting for the patterns of firm dynamics as well as the connection between market structure and institutions and the relationship between firm dynamics and economic growth. This literature has recently been reviewed by Davis and

Haltiwanger (1999), Bartelsman and Doms (2000), Foster et al. (2001), and Bartelsman et al. (2004, 2005). Rather than repeat these extensive reviews, this chapter draws on the data projects and related analysis from Bartelsman et al. (2005), Davis et al. (2006a, 2006b), Haltiwanger (2006), and Haltiwanger, Scarpetta, and Schweiger (2006). Two separate but related data projects, discussed immediately below, underlie these papers. The first enables analysis of job dynamics in the United States, and the second enables harmonized analysis of job flows as well as the connection between reallocation and productivity dynamics in 16 economies.

## Job Flows: Data and Measurement

The analysis here draws on two distinct but related sets of data. First, the longitudinal business database (LBD) represents a comprehensive data set for all firms and establishments in the United States from 1976 to 2001. The statistics used here are from analyses in Davis et al. (2006a, 2006b) and Haltiwanger (2006).

The second set of analysis of job flows draws from a harmonized firm-level database that involves 16 industrial, developing, and emerging economies (Germany, Finland, France, Italy, Portugal, the United Kingdom, the United States, Estonia, Hungary, Latvia, Slovenia, Argentina, Brazil, Chile, Colombia, and Mexico).[4] The data collection, conducted by local experts actively participating in each of the countries, involved harmonizing key concepts to the extent possible (such as entry and exit of firms, job creation and destruction, and the unit of measurement), as well as defining common methods to compute the indicators (see Bartelsman et al. [2005] for details). One important limitation of these harmonized data is that they are based on registers, censuses, and surveys for the formal sector. Self-employed and/or informal sector workers are not included. A brief discussion of the potential role of the self-employed is presented in a later section, but for now these statistics should be interpreted in relation to the formal sector.

The empirical results focus on measuring business dynamics via job flows, defined as follows. First we define the growth rate of employment for a business $j$ as:

$$g_{jt} = (E_{jt} - E_{jt-1})/X_{jt} \tag{1}$$

where $E_{jt}$ is employment for business $j$ for a time $t$, and $X_{jt} = .5(E_{jt} + E_{jt-1})$. As discussed in detail in Davis, Haltiwanger, and Schuh (1996), this

growth rate measure has several advantageous properties: (i) it accommodates entry and exit, (ii) it is symmetric for employment gains and losses,
and (iii) it is a second order approximation of the log first difference.[5]

Then, by using this growth rate measure, job creation and destruction
rates for businesses with characteristics $s$ (where this might be the total
economy or businesses defined by employer size or age) are defined
as follows:

$$JC_{st} = \sum_{g_{jt} \geq 0, j \in s} (X_{jt}/X_{st})g_{jt} \tag{2}$$

$$JD_{st} = \sum_{g_{jt} < 0, j \in s} (X_{jt}/X_{st})|g_{jt}| \tag{3}$$

where

$$X_{st} = \sum_{j \in s} X_{jt} \tag{4}$$

Job creation (JC) thus measures the gross employment gains from all
expanding businesses (including contribution from entry), and job
destruction (JD) measures the gross employment gains from all contracting businesses for employers of type $s$.[6] By construction, the net growth
rate (NET) for sector $s$ is given by the difference between creation and
destruction. That is,

$$NET_{st} = JC_{st} - JD_{st} \tag{5}$$

A summary measure of the total amount of job reallocation is given
by the following:

$$SUM_{st} = JC_{st} + JD_{st} \tag{6}$$

The total job reallocation rate (SUM) is a measure of the total rate of
all jobs reallocated in a period. Each of these concepts can be further
decomposed into the contribution from continuing businesses and the
contribution from entering and exiting businesses. Moreover, it is often
useful to create a measure of EXCESS job reallocation, which is measured as total job reallocation minus the absolute value of net growth.
This latter measure captures the job flows over and above those needed
to accommodate the net growth for the sector. These statistics can be

constructed for a variety of employer characteristics, including industry, size, and business age. Moreover, they can be constructed by country.

## Role of Employer Size and Age in Job Flows in the United States

To start, we present basic summary statistics by employer size, employer age, and employer size and age together. These statistics are from a comprehensive longitudinal database covering the entire U.S. private sector for a substantial period of time. Figure 6.1 presents statistics by employer size. Employer size is measured on the basis of the definition of $X_{jt}$ in the previous section. As Davis, Haltiwanger, and Schuh (1996) emphasize, using a measure such as $X_{jt}$ mitigates some of the regression to the mean problems with measures of employer size.[7] It is also worth emphasizing again that this measure is for firm size, not establishment size. Three firm size classes are considered: firms with fewer than 100 employees, firms with between 100 and 499 employees, and firms with more than 500 employees.

The top panel of figure 6.1 shows the patterns of net employment growth, job reallocation (SUM), firm turnover, and employment shares by employer size class.[8] Some basic and reasonably well-known patterns are confirmed. First, about half of all employment is with firms having fewer than 500 employees. Second, gross job flows as measured by job reallocation dwarf net growth rates. Third, job reallocation and firm turnover sharply decrease with employer size. Fourth, net growth exhibits a weak relationship with employer size. For this time period, there is a weak inverse relationship between the average net growth rate of firms with under 100 employees, at 2.27 percent, and the average net growth rate for firms with more than 500 employees, at 1.95 percent.

The lower panel of figure 6.1 shows the underlying patterns of job creation, job destruction, and entry (employment-weighted) and exit (employment-weighted). Almost half of the job creation and destruction for small firms comes from entry and exit. In contrast, less than one-third of the job creation and destruction of larger businesses comes from entry and exit.

Figure 6.2 reports analogous statistics for employer age. Employer age is measured in the LBD as the age of the oldest establishment. Two age classes are examined—firms younger than five years old and firms five or more years old.[9]

The patterns by this simple age breakdown are stark and striking. The net growth rate of young firms is much higher than that of mature firms.

**Figure 6.1. Job Flows by Employer Size**

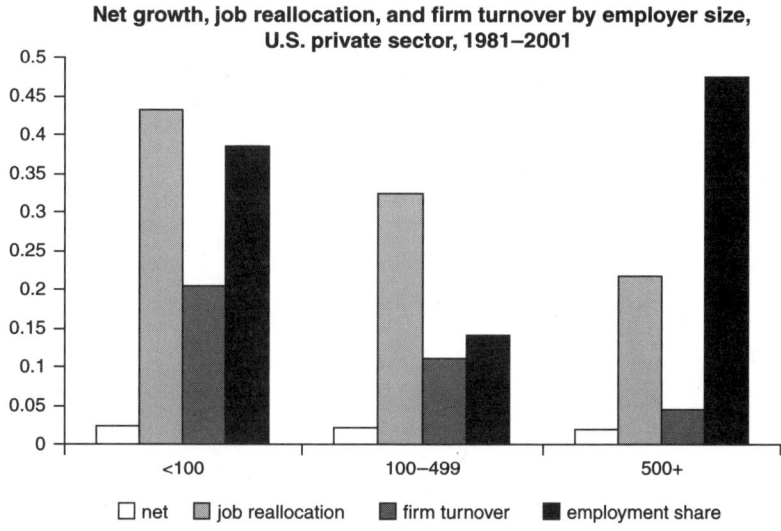

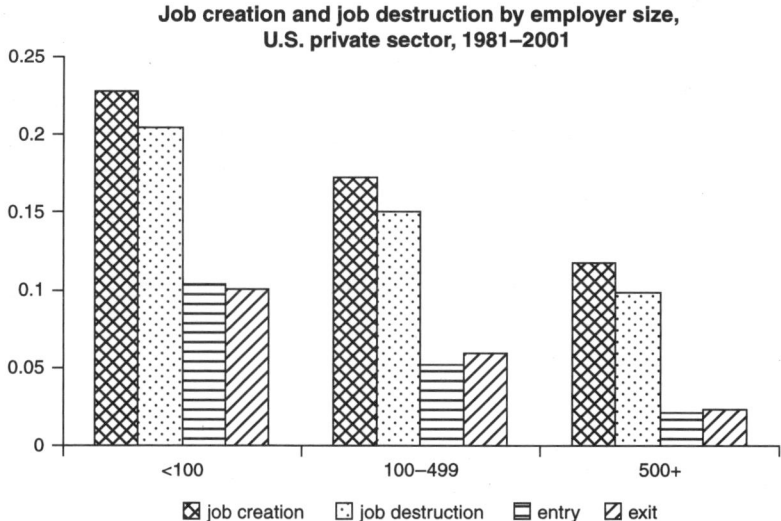

*Source:* Tabulations from LBD (based on Davis et al. [2006a]).

The annual average net growth rate of young firms is greater than 20 percent. The high net growth is accompanied by very high volatility, with firm turnover of almost 50 percent each year. These rapidly growing, volatile young firms account for a relatively small share of total employment in the United States (about 10 percent).

**Figure 6.2. Job Flows by Employer Age**

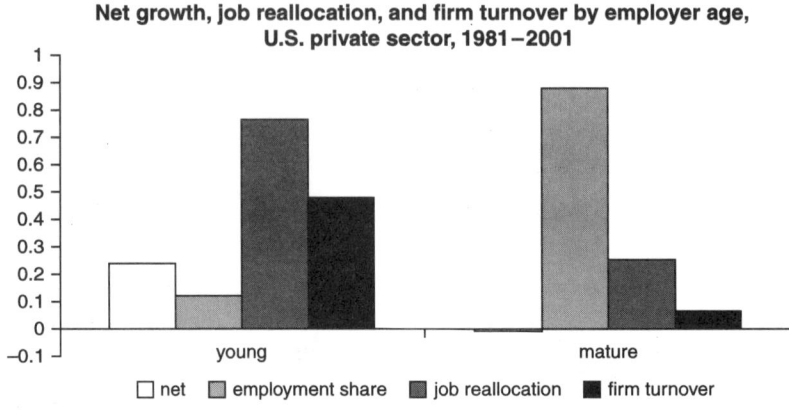

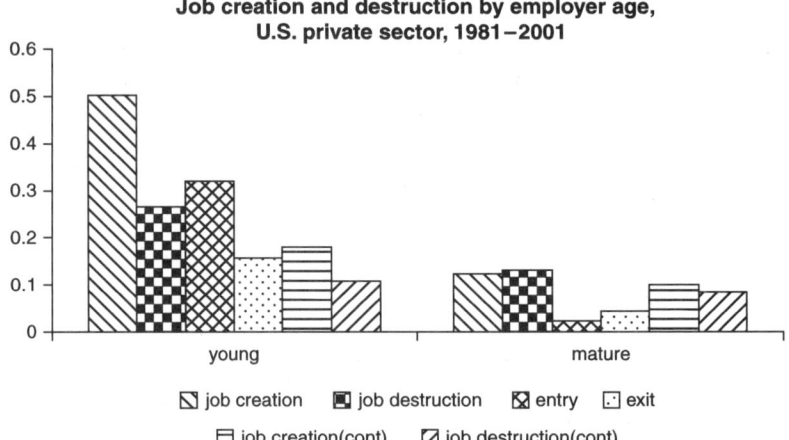

*Source:* Tabulations from LBD (based on Davis et al. [2006a]).

The lower panel shows the underlying patterns of job creation and destruction. This panel shows the job creation and destruction rates as well as the breakdown of contributions by continuing (cont) firms and entering and exiting firms. The young firms are striking in that more than 60 percent of the job creation is from entry and about half of the job destruction is due to exit. However, the high net growth rate and high volatility are also driven by young continuing firms, with job creation from continuing firms at almost 20 percent, and substantially above the job destruction rate of about 10 percent.

Mature firms, in contrast, have a modest negative net growth rate, with entry and exit accounting for only about 25 percent (still a large percentage) of the gross flows. Interestingly, the negative net growth is associated with the entry rate being less than the exit rate; but surviving mature firms exhibit positive but modest net growth.[10]

Figure 6.3 shows the job flow patterns of U.S. businesses with employer size and employer age interacted. Holding size constant, young businesses have much higher net growth rates than mature businesses, and are much more volatile. Again, holding size constant, the job creation and destruction of young businesses are driven in large part by entry and exit, but in considering the overall rates of job creation and

**Figure 6.3. Job Flows By Employer Size and Age**

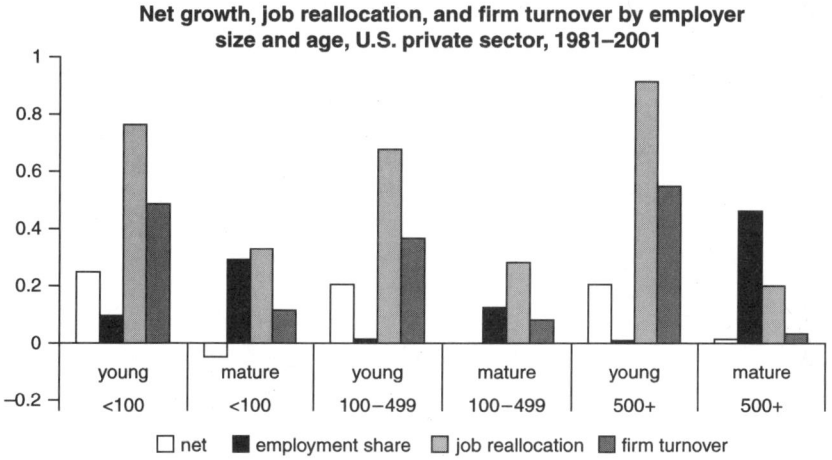

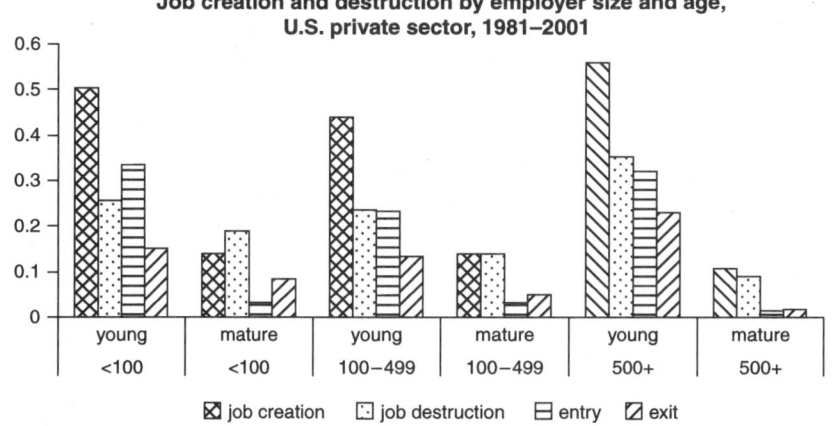

*Source:* Tabulations from LBD (based on Davis et al. [2006a]).

destruction relative to entry and exit, it is clear that young continuing businesses also exhibit considerable volatility.

Holding age constant, smaller businesses are more volatile, but there is no systematic relationship between employer size and net growth. For young businesses, size is negatively but modestly correlated with net employment growth. For mature businesses, the lowest net growth rate is for the smallest businesses.

It is also important to pay attention to employment shares in considering age and size effects together. The largest employment share is accounted for by large, mature businesses (more than 40 percent). The smallest employment share is accounted for by large, young businesses. That is, conditional on being young, most of the employment is with small businesses. Still, as noted, the high pace of volatility of medium and large, young firms is striking (even though they account for only a small share of activity).

Combining the insights of figures 6.1–6.3, the basic message that emerges is that for U.S. businesses, business age is a critical factor in accounting for differences in net growth and volatility. Employer size has more modest effects, even after controlling for age. In many ways, these patterns confirm findings in the existing literature for the United States focusing on the U.S. manufacturing sector.

What should we make of these patterns? First, it is clear from figures 6.1–6.3 and the existing literature that U.S. businesses exhibit high volatility, with the resulting high churning of jobs. Second, much but not all of this volatility is associated with the high volatility of young businesses via both high entry and exit rates for young businesses. Third, even for large, mature businesses, there is considerable volatility with a job reallocation rate of 20 percent (see figure 6.3). Much of that is driven by the reallocation among continuing firms, but it nevertheless represents considerable churning of jobs.

A key message of course is that job growth is very much tied to business entry and the growth of young businesses. An open question is how these job dynamics look in other countries around the world. We turn to that question in the next section.

## Job Flows in Advanced, Emerging, and Transition Economies

This section explores the main stylized facts emerging from our analysis across countries, sectors, and firm size: (i) the large magnitude of job flows in all countries; (ii) the significant role that firm entry and exit play in total job flows; (iii) the different job turnover across firms of different sizes; and (iv) the similarities in the industry ranking of job turnover across countries.

## Large Job Turnover in All Countries

Table 6.1 presents summary statistics for job flows across regions for the total economy. Figure 6.4 summarizes country-level job flows and compares them across countries.

**Table 6.1. Average Job Flows in the 1990s, Overall and by Region, Total Economy**

| Variable | Obs. | Mean | Std. dev. | Min. | Max. |
|---|---|---|---|---|---|
| **Overall** | | | | | |
| Job creation rate | 1048 | 0.147 | 0.067 | 0.000 | 0.647 |
| Job destruction rate | 1048 | 0.131 | 0.062 | 0.000 | 0.419 |
| Net employment growth | 1048 | 0.015 | 0.065 | −0.299 | 0.419 |
| Job reallocation rate | 1048 | 0.278 | 0.112 | 0.000 | 0.875 |
| Excess job reallocation rate | 1048 | 0.231 | 0.098 | 0.000 | 0.732 |
| Job creation rate (entry) | 1048 | 0.055 | 0.043 | 0.000 | 0.357 |
| Job destruction rate (exit) | 1048 | 0.046 | 0.029 | 0.000 | 0.216 |
| **OECD** | | | | | |
| Job creation rate | 448 | 0.127 | 0.046 | 0.033 | 0.288 |
| Job destruction rate | 448 | 0.127 | 0.060 | 0.029 | 0.411 |
| Net employment growth | 448 | 0.000 | 0.046 | −0.282 | 0.148 |
| Job reallocation rate | 448 | 0.254 | 0.096 | 0.072 | 0.570 |
| Excess job reallocation rate | 448 | 0.223 | 0.085 | 0.058 | 0.472 |
| Job creation rate (entry) | 448 | 0.045 | 0.030 | 0.003 | 0.195 |
| Job destruction rate (exit) | 448 | 0.045 | 0.028 | 0.000 | 0.216 |
| **Latin America** | | | | | |
| Job creation rate | 300 | 0.148 | 0.061 | 0.033 | 0.431 |
| Job destruction rate | 300 | 0.140 | 0.066 | 0.041 | 0.419 |
| Net employment growth | 300 | 0.008 | 0.053 | −0.214 | 0.286 |
| Job reallocation rate | 300 | 0.288 | 0.114 | 0.086 | 0.785 |
| Excess job reallocation rate | 300 | 0.248 | 0.103 | 0.066 | 0.732 |
| Job creation rate (entry) | 300 | 0.056 | 0.040 | 0.000 | 0.227 |
| Job destruction rate (exit) | 300 | 0.053 | 0.032 | 0.003 | 0.152 |
| **Transition** | | | | | |
| Job creation rate | 300 | 0.174 | 0.088 | 0.000 | 0.647 |
| Job destruction rate | 300 | 0.128 | 0.061 | 0.000 | 0.385 |
| Net employment growth | 300 | 0.046 | 0.087 | −0.299 | 0.419 |
| Job reallocation rate | 300 | 0.303 | 0.123 | 0.000 | 0.875 |
| Excess job reallocation rate | 300 | 0.227 | 0.109 | 0.000 | 0.608 |
| Job creation rate (entry) | 300 | 0.070 | 0.056 | 0.000 | 0.357 |
| Job destruction rate (exit) | 300 | 0.039 | 0.025 | 0.000 | 0.135 |

*Source:* Haltiwanger, Scarpetta, and Schweiger (2006).

**Figure 6.4. Decomposition of Job Creation and Destruction by Continuing, Entering, and Exiting Firms, 1990s, Total Economy and Manufacturing**

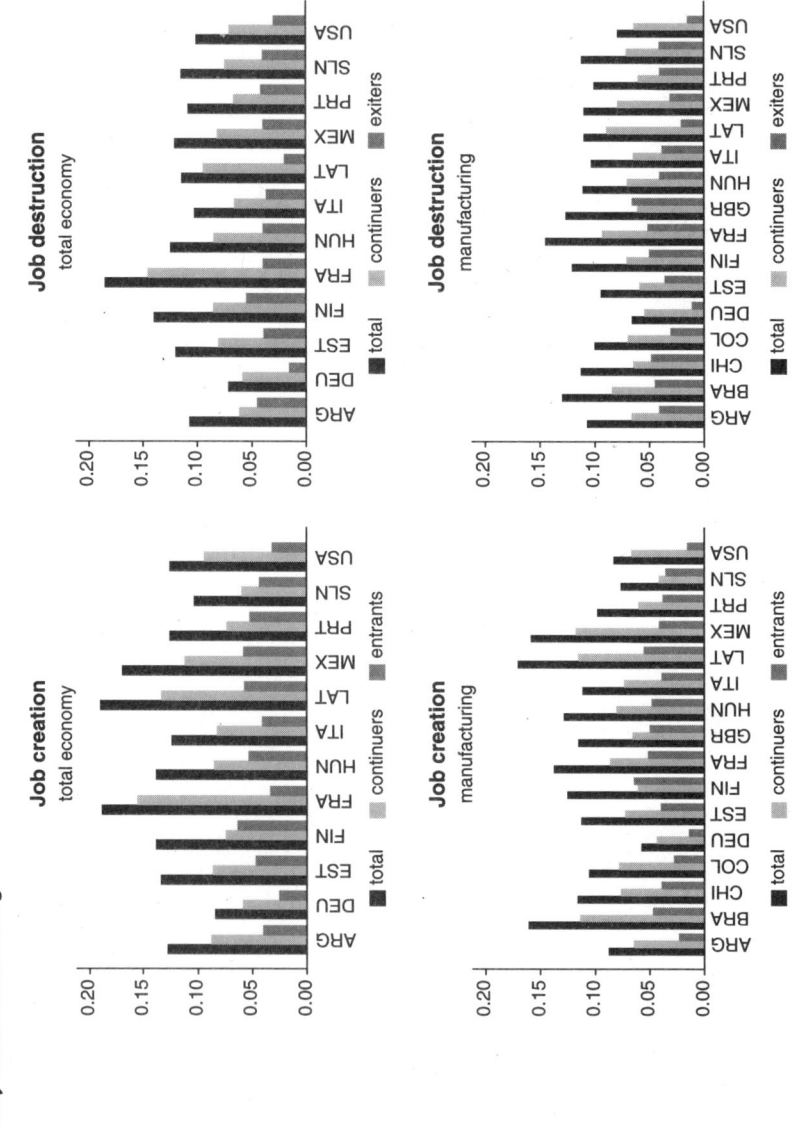

*Source:* Haltiwanger, Scarpetta, and Schweiger (2006).
ARG = Argentina, BRA = Brazil, CHI = Chile, COL = Colombia, DEU = Germany, EST = Estonia, FIN = Finland, FRA = France, GBR = Great Britain, HUN = Hungary, ITA = Italy, LAT = Latvia, MEX = Mexico, PRT = Portugal, SLN = Slovenia, USA = United States of America.

The first noticeable fact emerging from this cross-country comparison is the large magnitude of job flows in all countries. As the figures in table 6.1 show, gross job flows (the sum of job creation and job destruction) range from about 25 percent of total employment on average in the Organisation for Economic Co-operation and Development (OECD) countries, to 29 percent in Latin American countries, and to about 30 percent in the transition economies. By contrast, net employment changes were very modest if not nil in the OECD and the Latin America samples, whereas the transition economies, after the substantial job losses of the early phases of the transition, recorded a significant net job growth in the period covered by the data.

### Firm Dynamics Play a Major Role in Total Job Flows

The second main stylized fact emerging from the analysis of job flows is the strong contribution played by the creative destruction process. Indeed, entering and exiting firms account for about 30 to 40 percent of total job flows (these percentages are generated in Table 6.1 or Figure 6.4 by dividing, for example, the job creation rate from entry by the total job creation rate). In the OECD sample, the entry of new firms played a particularly strong role in total job creation in Finland in the 1990s (46 and 51 percent of total job creation in the total economy and in manufacturing, respectively), in Slovenia (42 and 46 percent of total job creation), and in Portugal (41 and 38 percent of total job creation). At the same time, the exit of obsolete firms also accounted for a significant fraction of overall job destruction, particularly so in Argentina (42 and 38 percent of total job destruction), Finland (39 and 41 percent of total job destruction), and Portugal (38 and 40 percent of total job destruction). In transition countries, entry was more important in the early years of transition and exit in the second half of the 1990s, both at the level of the total economy and in manufacturing.[11]

The large job flows in the transition countries are not surprising. The process of transition started in the early 1990s, and it included the downsizing of existing firms as well as new firms emerging as the economies were moving toward a market economy. Indeed, 40.2 percent of jobs were created by entering firms in transition countries, compared with 35.4 percent in the OECD countries. In addition, job destruction due to exit represented 35.4 percent of total job destruction in the OECD countries, but only 30.5 percent in transition countries. Findings are similar if we focus only on sectors in manufacturing.

### Analysis of Variance

The data on job flows in Haltiwanger, Scarpetta, and Schweiger (2006) exploit not only between-country variation but also within-country variation across industry and size classes. Exploring how the job flows vary by industry and size both within and between countries provides insights into the driving forces for job flows but also provides perspective on what factors might impede efficient reallocation across countries.

Table 6.2 presents the analysis of variance of job flows for the total economy and for manufacturing samples. Industry, size, country, and the combined effect of industry and size (interaction term industry size) are examined, and in addition, analysis of variance is differentiated by region. It is noticeable that technological and market structure characteristics that are reflected in the industry-specific effect explain only 6.8 percent of variation in overall cross-country gross job reallocation (although they account for a higher share in Latin America). By contrast, differences in the size structure of firms explain as much as 40 percent of the total variation in cross-country gross job reallocation in all regions, and played an even more important role in transition countries in the beginning of the 1990s. This fact is again in accordance with the characteristics of transition. Even country effects explain more of the variation in gross job reallocation than industry effects, except in Latin America, so even though there are similarities among countries within a region, there is still variation among them. Overall, the combined industry and size effects can explain the bulk of the variation in gross job reallocation: 55.6 percent overall, 55.8 percent in OECD countries, 73.3 percent in Latin America, and 72.3 percent in transition countries.

Gross job reallocation consists of job creation and job destruction, so we now turn to these two categories of job flows for further insight. We also further decompose them into job creation by new firms and by incumbents and job destruction by exiting firms and by those that survive but downsize.[12] A number of interesting features emerge:

- *Industry effects*. Industry effects explain about 7 percent of variation in job creation, and 6 percent of variation in job destruction, but there are significant differences among the three regions. Industry effects account for a much larger share of the overall variation (31 percent) in job creation in Latin America, slightly less than half of that in OECD countries, and only 7 percent in transition countries. In the early phases of transition, the creation of jobs occurred across all industries. Job destruction was more concentrated in certain industries

**Table 6.2. Analysis of Variance, Total Economy**

| | Job creation | Job destruction | Net employment growth | Gross job reallocation | Excess job reallocation | Job creation—entry | Job destruction—exit |
|---|---|---|---|---|---|---|---|
| **Industry effects** | | | | | | | |
| All | 0.0670 | 0.0613 | 0.0554 | 0.0675 | 0.0538 | 0.0164 | 0.0500 |
| OECD | 0.1492 | 0.0892 | 0.1164 | 0.1104 | 0.0509 | 0.0229 | 0.0706 |
| Latin America | 0.3076 | 0.1438 | 0.1568 | 0.2327 | 0.1655 | 0.1159 | 0.1049 |
| Transition (1990s) | 0.0644 | 0.0931 | 0.1525 | 0.0341 | 0.0877 | 0.0486 | 0.0938 |
| Transition (late 1990s) | 0.0731 | 0.0665 | 0.1350 | 0.0344 | 0.0790 | 0.0399 | 0.0827 |
| **Size effects** | | | | | | | |
| All | 0.3003 | 0.4100 | 0.0021 | 0.4706 | 0.4591 | 0.4325 | 0.3373 |
| OECD | 0.3027 | 0.3738 | 0.0605 | 0.4139 | 0.4468 | 0.4439 | 0.3127 |
| Latin America | 0.2142 | 0.6300 | 0.2557 | 0.4777 | 0.5093 | 0.5950 | 0.7000 |
| Transition (1990s) | 0.5400 | 0.2861 | 0.1443 | 0.6149 | 0.4706 | 0.4858 | 0.1236 |
| Transition (late 1990s) | 0.4309 | 0.2488 | 0.0708 | 0.5268 | 0.4945 | 0.4412 | 0.1441 |
| **Country effects** | | | | | | | |
| All | 0.2138 | 0.1252 | 0.1975 | 0.1648 | 0.1435 | 0.1453 | 0.1996 |
| OECD | 0.1576 | 0.2009 | 0.1113 | 0.2019 | 0.1885 | 0.1253 | 0.2829 |
| Latin America | 0.3041 | 0.0419 | 0.1808 | 0.1588 | 0.1276 | 0.1133 | 0.0255 |
| Transition (1990s) | 0.0570 | 0.0867 | 0.0974 | 0.0512 | 0.0865 | 0.0653 | 0.2031 |
| Transition (late 1990s) | 0.0997 | 0.0445 | 0.0681 | 0.0851 | 0.0933 | 0.0645 | 0.1719 |
| **Industry*size effects** | | | | | | | |
| All | 0.3861 | 0.4964 | 0.0904 | 0.5558 | 0.5263 | 0.4624 | 0.4097 |
| OECD | 0.4888 | 0.5041 | 0.2421 | 0.5579 | 0.5215 | 0.5018 | 0.4053 |
| Latin America | 0.5574 | 0.8079 | 0.5062 | 0.7326 | 0.6998 | 0.7364 | 0.8478 |
| Transition (1990s) | 0.6856 | 0.4685 | 0.3998 | 0.7233 | 0.6186 | 0.5956 | 0.3004 |
| Transition (late 1990s) | 0.5978 | 0.4736 | 0.3417 | 0.6692 | 0.6493 | 0.5676 | 0.3189 |

*Source:* Haltiwanger, Scarpetta, and Schweiger (2006); the figures are for the unbalanced panel.

in OECD countries and especially so in Latin America: 15 percent of variation in job destruction in Latin America can be explained by industry effects, but only 9 percent in OECD countries.

- *Size effects.* In the case of both job creation and job destruction, size effects alone account for a significant share of the total variation (30 and 41 percent, respectively). Looking at results by region reveals that in transition countries, size effects account for 54 percent of variation in job creation but only 29 percent of variation in job destruction. In Latin America, the results are the opposite: the size effects can account for 63 percent of job destruction, but for only 21 percent of job creation.

- *Role of the entry and exit of firms.* Size heterogeneity plays a particularly strong role in explaining the variation of job creation by new firms and the job destruction by exiting firms. Size heterogeneity is particularly important in Latin America, in which it accounts for 60 percent of job creation by new firms, and 70 percent of job destruction by exiting firms. In the OECD countries, size heterogeneity plays a smaller role in both job creation and job destruction by entering and exiting firms. In the transition economies, there is a strong difference between job creation and destruction. The variation of job creation by entry is strongly influenced by size heterogeneity, whereas the importance of size effects in job destruction by exit is relatively smaller.

How can these different sources of variability of job flows be interpreted? Not surprisingly, in all regions size heterogeneity looms large among new firms, depending on market conditions but also on regulations that may affect the optimal size of entry. This seems to be the case particularly in Latin America, in which industries with many new microentrants coexist with those in which entry size is larger. But size heterogeneity also explains a significant part of the variance in job destruction by firm exit: some sectors see large failures of small, young businesses, whereas others see the decline of more mature firms of larger size. By contrast, in transition economies, there is more variability in the size structure of new firms than there is in the size structure of those that exit the market. A large number of new activities entered the market filling different niches of activities that were largely underdeveloped during the period proceeding transition, whereas job destruction involved firms of different sizes more evenly, with the closure of many large, obsolete firms as well as of many relatively newer, small ventures. It is also noticeable that in the transition economies, country effects account for 20 percent of variation in job destruction by exiting firms, but only 6.5 percent of variation in job creation by entering firms. That is suggestive of the different pace of enterprise restructuring and the impact on firm closure and downsizing.[13]

To summarize, the analysis of variance of job flows suggests a significant role for size composition—a factor that was not considered in previous studies—and differences both across regions and within each region. Industry effects seem to play a relatively smaller role in explaining cross-country differences in job flows.

Comparing these results with those for the United States, it is useful to recall, first, that size is closely related to age, and second, that the young and small U.S. businesses play a critical role in job dynamics with both high average growth and considerable volatility.

### Summing Up

In all countries under review, job flows are large. In all countries under review, the entry and exit of businesses play an important role in accounting for these flows. In considering the variation across country, industry, and size, size effects play a major role in accounting for the variation. Small (and presumably young) businesses are inherently more volatile. Industry and size effects together account for more than half of the variation across countries, industries, and size classes. This large role for industry and size effects tells us there are some fundamental factors involved in the types of shocks and adjustments that affect businesses in specific industry and size cells that help account for firm dynamics. However, even after accounting for the interaction of size and industry effects, is considerable variation remains unaccounted for, representing differences across countries in the nature of the variation. An open question is: to what extent is this variation accounted for by differences in market structure and institutions across countries? A related important question is: to what extent does this churning of firms and jobs contribute to productivity growth? We turn to that question in the next section.

### Effects of Creative Destruction on Productivity

Key open questions are: What is the contribution of the creative destruction process to productivity growth? How does this vary across countries? How do market structure and institutions affect the productivity-enhancing nature of the creative destruction process? Can we account for cross-country differences in the level and growth of productivity via the efficiency

of the creative destruction process? These are big and difficult questions
that still remain open. Bartelsman et al. (2005) discuss them in detail, as
well as the difficulties encountered in addressing them. In this chapter, we
borrow from one aspect of that analysis focusing on a dimension of the
issue that arguably yields simple and robust comparisons across countries.
The approach is to ask the question—are resources allocated efficiently in
a sector or country in the cross section at a given point in time? Dynamics
can also be examined here, to the extent that the nature of the efficiency
of the cross-sectional allocation of businesses can vary over time.

This approach is based on a simple cross-sectional decomposition of
productivity growth developed by Olley and Pakes (1996). They note
that in the cross-section, the level of productivity ($P$) for a sector at a
point in time ($t$) can be decomposed as follows:

$$P_t = (1/N_t)\sum_i P_{it} + \sum_i \Delta\theta_{it}\Delta P_{it} \qquad (7)$$

where $N$ is the number of businesses in the sector, $\Delta$ is the operator that
represents the cross-sectional deviation of the firm-level measure from the
industry simple average, and $\theta_{it}$ is the market share of firm $i$ at time $t$. The
simple interpretation of this decomposition is that aggregate productivity
can be decomposed into two terms, involving the unweighted average of
firm-level productivity, and a cross term that reflects the cross-sectional
efficiency of the allocation of activity. The cross term captures allocative
efficiency because it reflects the extent to which firms with greater efficiency have a greater market share.

This simple decomposition is very easy to implement, and essentially
involves just measuring the unweighted average productivity *versus* the
weighted average productivity. Measurement problems make comparisons of the levels of either of these measures across sectors or countries
very problematic, but taking the difference between these two measures
reflects a form of a difference-in-difference approach. Beyond measurement advantages, this approach also has the related virtue that theoretical
predictions are more straightforward. Distortions to market structure
and institutions unambiguously imply that the difference between
weighted and unweighted productivity (or equivalently, the cross term)
should be smaller than in the absence of distortions.[14]

With these remarks in mind, we examine figure 6.5, which shows the
gap between weighted and unweighted average productivity for a sample
of countries. For virtually all countries, the gap is positive, suggesting that

**Figure 6.5. The Gap between Weighted and Unweighted Labor Productivity, 1990s**

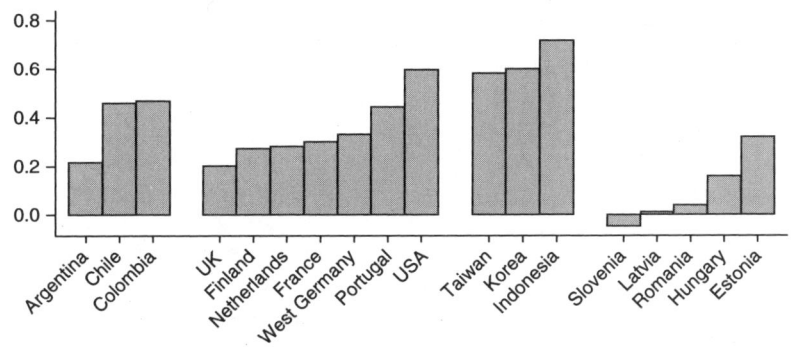

Data for Hungary, Indonesia and Romania use Three-Year Differencing.
Excluding Brazil and Venezuela.

*Source:* Haltiwanger, Scarpetta, and Schweiger (2006).

resources are allocated to more productive businesses in these countries. The South East Asian economies show the largest gap, followed by the United States. The Latin American countries, except Argentina, show higher productivity boosts through resource allocation than the EU but lower than the Asian countries. The transition economies generally are weaker in regard to this measure of allocative efficiency. For many countries, the gap is positive and large. For the Asian economies and the United States, the allocative efficiency term accounts for more than 50 percent of productivity. In the EU, the productivity boost is smaller— roughly 25 percent.

The findings in figure 6.5 are striking, and suggest that this measurement approach has great potential in a cross-country context. Moreover, the allocative efficiency measures can be computed for different years or for specific industries and/or other classifications of firms, suggesting that a pooled-country, firm-type data set of allocative efficiency measures would be valuable for further analysis. Note, however, that the allocative efficiency measures are not without problems and limitations. A key problem is that the measures by construction do not permit decomposing the contribution of entering, exiting, and continuing businesses. As such, in an analysis of the impact of institutions on reallocation and productivity dynamics, these allocative efficiency measures cannot be used to investigate the impact of institutions on such measures of firm dynamics, and in turn the contribution of those effects on productivity. Measurement error will also cloud the interpretation of the allocative efficiency measures. Classical measurement error in productivity at the microlevel, that is, uncorrelated with market share, will tend to drive the allocative efficiency to zero. Classical measurement error in productivity that is also correlated with market share (put differently, classical measurement error in output measures at the microlevel) will work in the opposite direction.

## Missing Pieces—Self-Employment and the Informal Sector

One of the limitations of the analysis of firm dynamics for the advanced, emerging, and transition economies is that it is limited to the formal sector and/or to firms with employees. In virtually all economies, an important alternative source of employment is self-employment. Moreover, in some economies, even in businesses with "employees," the businesses are not registered and/or some of the employees are not registered. This issue looms large especially for emerging economies, because the size of the informal sector is purported to be large. Moreover, neither the nature of business dynamics in the informal sector nor the connection between the formal and informal sector is well understood.

It is well beyond the scope of this chapter to explore the role of the informal sector in this context. However, recent data on infrastructure development and related analysis for the United States raise some interesting questions on the relationship between self-employment and firm dynamics. One of the key messages from the findings in the previous sections is that young and small firms exhibit high average growth and are very volatile. The high growth and volatility of young firms is driven in part by entry and exit and also by the rapid but volatile growth of continuing young firms.

Given the importance of young firms in accounting for growth and volatility, it is of interest to understand their entry dynamics on a variety of dimensions. Recent analysis (e.g., Davis et al. 2006a) has highlighted the role of microbusinesses without employees as being part of the testing ground for new employer businesses. Figure 6.6 shows why such microbusinesses are likely to be important for understanding the dynamics of young and small businesses. Of the roughly 20 million businesses in the United States, about 75 percent of them do not have employees. Most of the latter are sole proprietors. The 15 million or so nonemployer businesses are interesting in their own right, simply because of their high number, and because in a related way these reflect individuals who have at least some self-employment income. Of course, many of these

**Figure 6.6. Comparisons of Employer and Nonemployer Business**

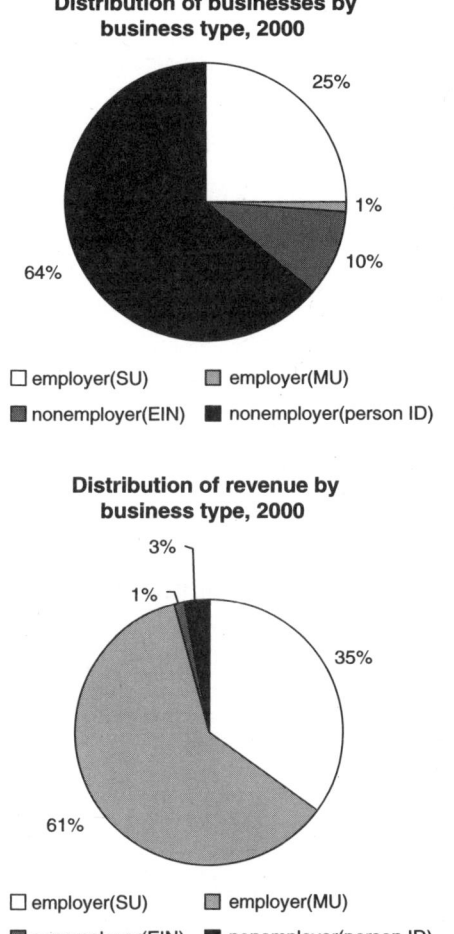

### Distribution of businesses by business type, 2000

25%

1%

10%

64%

☐ employer(SU)          ▨ employer(MU)
▨ nonemployer(EIN)   ■ nonemployer(person ID)

### Distribution of revenue by business type, 2000

3%

1%

35%

61%

☐ employer(SU)          ▨ employer(MU)
■ nonemployer(EIN)   ■ nonemployer(person ID)

*Source:* Tabulations from ILBD (based on Davis et al. [2006b]).
*Note:* SU = single unit establishment firm; MU = multiunit establishment firm; EIN = nonemployer that is partnership or corporation; person ID = nonemployer, sole proprietor firm.

microbusinesses are truly micro in that their share of revenue is quite small. About 96 percent of gross revenue from U.S. businesses, according to the lower panel of figure 6.6, derives from businesses with employees, and most of the latter comes from multiestablishment firms.

Only a small fraction of the large number of microbusinesses transit to employer businesses, but they account for a substantial fraction of employer entrants. Put differently, a substantial fraction of young employer businesses have a prehistory as nonemployer businesses. Figure 6.7 shows that for a selected set of industries, about 30 percent of young employer firms have a prehistory as nonemployers, and about 20 percent of the revenue of young employer firms is earned by firms that were at one time nonemployers.

How might these findings be relevant for emerging and transition economies? Figures 6.1–3 already demonstrated the importance of young and small businesses for job dynamics in the United States. By construction, these dynamics are closely linked with firm and establishment entry (of employer businesses). Figure 6.7 in turn suggests that a potentially important part of entry of employer businesses are businesses that have a history of having been "microbusinesses" without any employees.

Because barriers to entry are likely greater in emerging and transition economies owing to poor market structure and institutions, the transitional dynamics in figures 6.1–3 and figure 6.7 may be stifled or distorted in emerging and transition economies. Put differently, it may be that the barriers to entry prevent those micro "informal" businesses from making the

**Figure 6.7. Young Employers (0–3 years) with Prehistory as Nonemployers**

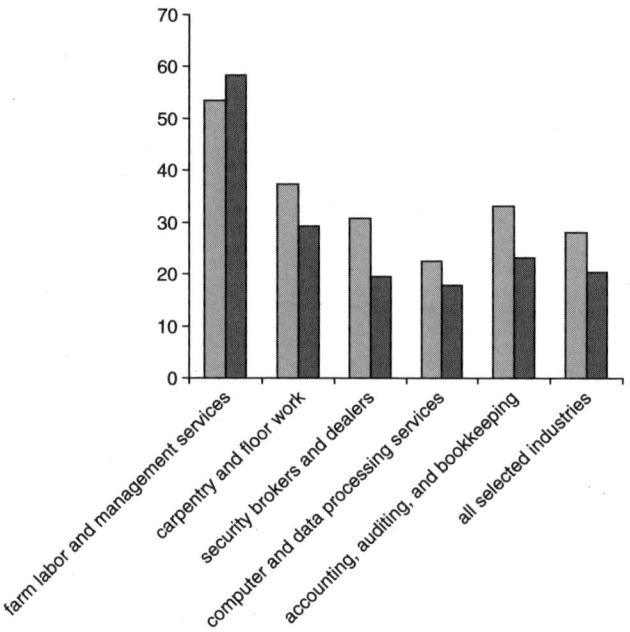

*Source:* Tabulations from ILBD (based on Davis et al. [2006b]).

transitions shown in figure 6.7 and in turn prevent the young employer businesses from playing the vital role that they play in the United States.

## Concluding Remarks

This chapter has reviewed key findings on job dynamics in the United States and around the world. In addition, it has reviewed some of the emerging findings that suggest that the constant churning of firms and jobs in advanced economies such as the United States is productivity enhancing. Key themes that emerge from this evidence include the role of microbusinesses without employees, the role of entering employer businesses (some of which grew out of microbusinesses), and the post-entry dynamics of young businesses. Young and small businesses in the United States play key roles in job and productivity growth. The open question is whether poor market structure and institutions stifle or distort the dynamics of micro, young, and small businesses, and whether such distortions have adverse impacts on both the labor market and business performance.

The discussion in this chapter reflects an overview of the findings and implications from recent studies using firm-level data in the United States and for other advanced economies, as well as for emerging and transition economies. Given that this is a burgeoning literature, this chapter is not a comprehensive review of the literature. Among the missing pieces, two deserve attention here. One is the role of the informal economy. This topic is approached indirectly through evidence of the role of self-employment as a source of both jobs and firm startups. The discussion focuses on the finding for the United States that self-employed workers who are successful can and do often make the transition to businesses with employees. The speculation is that perhaps this transition is much more difficult in emerging and transition economies.

A second missing issue is the impact on workers. It is clear that the churning of firms and jobs implies a degree of job instability in the United States and other advanced economies. The United States accommodates this churning with a high rate of job-to-job flows (estimates suggest about 25 percent of the churning is accommodated via direct job-to-job flows). Moreover, unemployment durations are quite short in the United States, which also keeps the impact in regard to lost activity and the adverse impact on workers lower. Of course, even in the United States, workers who are displaced can and do suffer adverse consequences. It is precisely this job instability, along with concerns about its adverse consequences, that has led to the adoption of many labor regulations around the world to regulate separations (via severance pay and/or outright prohibition of separations for certain types of workers and contracts). Although these policies are well intentioned, on both theoretical and empirical grounds, the regulations can have a perverse effect in that taxes on job destruction stifle the incentives for job creation. Still, emerging and transition economies are continually struggling to find the right mix of institutions to permit flexibility but also to provide a safety net for workers.

At the end of the day, drawing policy implications is difficult, and not simply because this type of empirical work is in its infancy. The problem is that it is difficult to evaluate the distortions to allocative efficiency simply by examining indicators of the pace of restructuring or even by looking at more sophisticated relationships between restructuring and measures of allocative efficiency (as in the Olley-Pakes decompositions of productivity). The challenge is that distortions may yield too much rather than too little reallocation, and in a related way distortions may have an impact on different margins. A country, for example, may look reasonably good in regard to the Olley-Pakes allocative efficiency component because the distortions are not affecting the allocation of resources among existing businesses, but they may be affecting the market selection margin. To be able to make stronger inferences about the relevant distortions, more structure is required to interpret the patterns from firm-level data discussed in this chapter. One way to think about all of the patterns discussed here is that they are empirical moments that can be used to calibrate, estimate, and analyze structural models of the allocative efficiency process. There has been recent progress along those lines (see Restuccia and Rogerson 2003; Hsieh and Klenow 2006; and Bartelsman, Haltiwanger, and Scarpetta 2006). The promising aspects of this latter approach are that these studies are able to use the empirical moments and are helping with their interpretation. For example, Bartelsman, Haltiwanger, and Scarpetta (2006) show that although distortions can affect different margins, distortions do tend to reduce the Olley-Pakes allocative efficiency component of productivity in sensible ways. Such findings highlight the need to bring the theory and empirics of reallocation dynamics together in this burgeoning literature by using firm-level data. In future research, a high priority should be given to the question whether market structure and institutions stifle or distort the dynamics of businesses and have adverse impacts on both the labor market and business performance.

## Notes

1. See, for example, Foster et al. (2001), Bartelsman et al. (2005), and Bartelsman and Doms (2000).

2. For example, many theoretical papers, such as Lucas (1978), Jovanovic (1982), and Pakes and Ericson (1996), emphasize the role of managerial ability.

3. The hold-up problem is a term used to describe a situation where two parties refrain from cooperating, although this would be more efficient, because they are concerned about giving the other party increased bargaining power and thereby reducing their own profits.

4. The database also includes Indonesia, South Korea, and Taiwan (China) as well as the Netherlands, Canada, Denmark, Romania, and Venezuela, but annual data on job flows are not available for these countries or are not fully reliable.

5. See Davis, Haltiwanger, and Schuh (1996) and Tornqvist, Vartia, and Vartia (1985) for further discussion.

6. As has become standard in the literature, in equation 3 job destruction is measured as a positive statistic, and because this is based on firms with negative growth rates, we use the weighted average of the absolute value of growth rates.

7. These are the averages across the 1981–2001 period. Regression to the mean problems are the most problematic using base size measures of size classes. The Bureau of Labor Statistics (BLS) method of dynamic sizing overcomes many of the problems associated with transitory shocks. We note that the basic patterns that we focus on here also appear to hold with the Business Employment Dynamics (BED) using dynamic sizing methods.

8. These are the averages across the 1981–2001 period. The 1981–2001 period is used because it permits measuring young (less than five yeas old) and mature firms (five or more years old) on a consistent basis.

9. Given left censoring in the LBD in 1975, all of the tabulations in this paper using the LBD start in 1981.

10. Of course, the higher exit than entry rate for mature firms is almost by construction because in some ways it is surprising to see any "entry" for mature firms. It turns out that there are some mature firms that have periods of inactivity, so entry should actually be interpreted as going from zero to positive activity from year $t-1$ to $t$. Alternatively, there are some new firms with old establishments. For the most part, such entities would not be measured as new firms, but in some cases that might happen.

11. This was especially so in Slovenia. A great deal of entry occurred in the early 1990s because there were few private firms before that; exit did not keep up with that early on and was relatively low compared with OECD and other transition countries.

12. We report results only for job creation by new firms and job destruction by existing firms; other results are available on request.

13. See Haltiwanger and Vodopivec (2003) and the World Bank (2004).

14. However, even here there needs to be caution because distortions may act on different margins. It may be that distortions affect market selection more than allocative efficiency in an existing group of firms. Thus, a country with distortions may not have such a poor showing on this measure but may on alternative measures.

## Bibliography

Acs, Z., C. Armington, and A. Robb. 1999. "Measures of Job Flow Dynamics in the U.S. Economy." Mimeo. http://www.sba.gov/advo/research/rs192tot.pdf

Aghion, P., and P. Howitt. 1998. *Endogenous Growth Theory.* Cambridge, MA: MIT Press.

Aw, B. Y., X. Chen, and M. J. Roberts. 2001. "Firm-Level Evidence on Productivity Differentials and Turnover in Taiwanese Manufacturing." *Journal of Development Economics* 66 (1): 51–86.

Baily, M., C. Hulten, and D. Campbell. 1992. "Productivity Dynamics in Manufacturing Plants." In *Brookings Papers on Economic Activity, Microeconomics,* 187–267. Washington, DC: Brookings Institution.

Bartelsman, E. J., and M. Doms. 2000. "Understanding Productivity: Lessons from Longitudinal Data." Finance and Economics Discussion Series No. 2000-19. Board of Governors of the Federal Reserve System.

Bartelsman, E., J. Haltiwanger, and S. Scarpetta. 2004. "Microeconomic Evidence of Creative Destruction in Industrial and Developing Countries." Policy Research Working Paper No. 3464. World Bank, Washington, DC.

———. 2005. "Measuring and Analyzing Cross-Country Differences in Firm Dynamics." mimeo. See http://193.205.83.2/~confeco/bartelsman.pdf

———. 2006 "Cross-Country Differences in Productivity: The Role of Allocative Efficiency." Mimeo. Mimeo. See http://www.dime-eu.org/Bartelsman_et-ali_paper

Bentolila, S, and G. Bertola. 1990. "Firing Costs and Labor Demand: How Bad Is Eurosclerosis?" *Review of Economic Studies* 57 (3): 381–402.

Bertola, G. 1992. "Labor Turnover Costs and Average Labor Demand." *Journal of Labour Economics* 10 (4): 389–411.

Bertola, G., and R. Rogerson. 1997. "Institutions and Labor Reallocation." *European Economic Review* 41 (6): 1147–71.

Boeri, T. 1999. "Enforcement of Employment Security Regulations, On-the-Job Search and Unemployment Duration." *European Economic Review* 43 (1): 65–89.

Caballero, R. J., and M. L. Hammour. 2000a. "Institutions, Restructuring, and Macroeconomic Performance." NBER Working Paper No. 7720. NBER (National Bureau of Economic Research), Cambridge, MA.

————. 2000b. "Creative Destruction and Development: Institutions, Crises, and Restructuring." NBER Working Paper No. 7849. NBER, Cambridge, MA.

Caballero, R. J., K. N. Cowan, E. M. R. A. Engel, and A. Micco. 2004. "Effective Labor Regulation and Microeconomic Flexibility." Cowles Foundation Discussion Paper No. 1480. Cowles Foundation, Yale University, New Haven, CT.

Classens, S., and L. Laeven. 2003. "Financial Development, Property Rights and Growth." *Journal of Finance* 58 (6): 2401–36.

Davis, S., and J. Haltiwanger. 1999. "On the Driving Forces Behind Cyclical Movements in Employment and Job Reallocation." *American Economic Review* 89 (5): 1234–58.

Davis, S., J. Haltiwanger, and S. Schuh. 1996. *Job Creation and Destruction*. Cambridge, MA: MIT Press.

Davis, S. J., J. Haltiwanger, R. Jarmin, and J. Miranda. 2006a. "Volatility and Dispersion in Business Growth Rates: Publicly Traded vs. Privately Held Firms." National Bureau for Economic Research (NBER) Working Paper 12354.

Davis, S. J., J. Haltiwanger, R. Jarmin, C. J. Krizan, J. Miranda, A. Nucci, and K. Sandusky. 2006b. "Measuring the Dynamics of Young and Small Businesses: Integrating the Employer and Nonemployer Universes." Centre for Economic Studies (CES) Working Paper No. 06-04.

Dunne, T., M. J. Roberts, and L. Samuelson. 1988. "Patterns of Firm Entry and Exit in U.S. Manufacturing Industries." *RAND Journal of Economics* 19 (4): 495–515.

————. 1989. "Plant Turnover and Gross Employment Flows in the U.S. Manufacturing Plants." *Journal of Labor Economics* 7 (1): 48–71.

EUROSTAT (Statistical Office of the European Communities). 1998. "Enterprises in Europe, Data 1994–95." 5th Report of the European Commission. European Commission, Brussels, Belgium.

Foster, L, J. Haltiwanger, and C. J. Krizan. 2001. "Aggregate Productivity Growth: Lessons from Microeconomic Evidence." In *New Developments in Productivity Analysis*, ed. E. Dean, M. Harper, and C. Hulten. Chicago, IL: University of Chicago Press.

————. 2002. "The Link Between Aggregate and Micro Productivity Growth: Evidence from Retail Trade." NBER Working Paper No. 9120. NBER, Cambridge, MA.

Griliches, Z., and H. Regev. 1996. "Firm Productivity in Israeli Industry 1979–1988." *Econometrica* 65: 175–203.

Gwartney, J., and R. Lawson. 2005. *Economic Freedom of the World*, Annual Report. Vancouver, B.C.: Fraser Institute.

Haltiwanger, J. 2006. "Entrepreneurship and Job Growth." Mimeo. See http://research.kauffman.org/cwp/ShowProperty/webCacheRepository/Doc uments/Haltiwanger_Jobs_May_2006.pdf

Haltiwanger, J., and M. Vodopivec. 2003. "Worker Flows, Job Flows and Firm Wage Policies: An Analysis of Slovenia." *Economics of Transition* 11 (2): 253–90.

Haltiwanger, J., S. Scarpetta, and M. Vodopivec. 2003. "How Institutions Affect Labor Market Outcomes: Evidence from Transition Countries." Mimeo. World Bank, Washington, DC.

Haltiwanger, J., S. Scarpetta, and H. Schweiger. 2006. "Assessing the Job Flows Across Countries: The Role of Industry, Size, and Regulations." Mimeo. World Bank, Washington, DC.

Heckman, J. J., and C. Pages, eds. 2004. *Law and Employment: Lessons from Latin America and the Caribbean.* NBER Conference Series Report. Chicago and London: University of Chicago Press.

Hsieh, C., and P. Klenow. 2006. "Misallocation and Manufacturing TFP in China and India." Mimeo. See http://www.econ.nyu.edu/cvstarr/seminars/klenow.pdf

Klapper, L., L. Laeven, and R. G. Rajan. 2004. "Business Environment and Firm Entry: Evidence from International Data." NBER Working Paper Series No. 10380. NBER, Cambridge, MA.

Jovanovic, B. 1982. "Selection and the Evolution of Industry." *Econometrica* 50 (3): 915–38.

Lucas, R.E. 1978. "On the Size Distribution of Business Firms." *The Bell Journal of Economics*, 9 (2): 2. Autumn/508–23.

Micco, A., and C. Pages. 2004. "Employment Protection and Gross Job Flows: A Difference-in-Difference Approach." Mimeo. See http://www-ilo-mirror.cor nell.edu/public/english/bureau/integration/download/publicat/4_3_344_wb-iadb_paper_on_employment_protection_and_gross_job_flows_pci_meet ing_june_2005.pdf

Mortensen, D. T., and C. A. Pissarides. 1999 "Job Reallocation, Employment Fluctuations and Unemployment." In *Handbook of Macroeconomics*, Vol. 1B, 1171–228. Amsterdam, New York, and Oxford: Elsevier Science, North-Holland.

———. "New Developments in Models of Search in the Labor Market." 1999. In *Handbook of Labor Economics*, Vol. 3B, 2567–627. Amsterdam, New York, and Oxford: Elsevier Science, North-Holland.

Nickell, S., and R. Layard. 1999. "Labor Market Institutions and Economic Performance." In *Handbook of Labor Economics*, Volume 3C, 3029–84. Amsterdam, New York, and Oxford: Elsevier Science, North-Holland.

Olley, G. S., and A. Pakes. 1996. "The Dynamics of Productivity in the Telecommunications Equipment Industry." *Econometrica* 64 (6): 1263–97.

Pakes A., R. Ericson. 1998. "Empirical Implications of Alternative Models of Firm Dynamics." *Journal of Economic Theory* 79 (1): 1–46.

Rajan, R. G., and L. Zingales. 1998. "Financial Dependence and Growth." *American Economic Review* 88 (3): 559–86.

Restuccia, D., and R. Rogerson. 2003. "Policy Distortions and Aggregate Productivity with Heterogeneous Plants." Mimeo. See http://ideas.repec.org/p/red/sed004/69.html

Tornqvist, L., P. Vartia, and Y. Vartia. 1985. "How Should Relative Change Be Measured?" *American Statistician* 39 (1): 43–6.

World Bank. 2004. "Improving the Investment Climate for Growth and Poverty Reduction." In *World Development Report 2005.* Washington, DC. World Bank.

# Index